Simple
SMART
Skills

Volume 2 (Win)

Winning With Windows™
Notebook™ 10 Software

Mike Palecek

SIMPLE SMART SKILLS
Volume 2
Winning With Windows™ Notebook™ 10 Software

PUBLISHING HISTORY
Lulu Press trade paperback edition –December 2008

ISBN-13: 978-0-557-01243-5 (pbk.)

Contents

1. – Notebook™ ideas...1

2. – Welcome Center – an Introduction............................8

3. – Thirtysomething tools...11

4. – Notebook Menus...53

5. – Object Menus...123

6. – Notebook Tabs..135

7. – Advanced Tools..172

8. – Index...219

1

Notebook™ ideas

Using SMART Technologies Notebook™ software for something like brainstorming can be surprisingly simple: touch the Full Screen Tool and your SMART Board™ is a multipage easel pad, complete with electronic ink. When your session is finished, go back to normal mode and print, using Control-P. Export to PDF and email participants your meeting notes. For some very satisfied users, that is all they will ever need to do with Notebook software.

But there is so much more to Notebook software. Simple SMART Skills: Volume 2, Winning With Windows™ Notebook™ 10 is a comprehensive guide to this powerful teaching tool. Hopefully, this book will become well-worn and dog-eared, a reliable reference in your quest toward effective multisensory communication and student engagement in your classroom.

Let's begin by viewing screen shots of Notebook software in action in the classroom:

Notebook Ideas

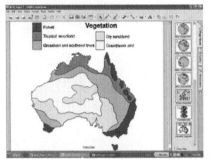

Replace your pull down maps with updated maps from the internet. Annotate over them.

Teach musical notation as part of music appreciation class.

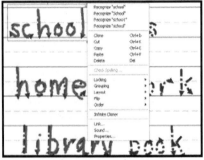

Have students practice handwriting and then convert it to text.

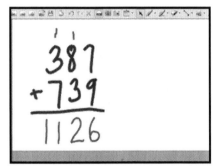

Have students demonstrate math problems.

Let students have fun and learn to make change by moving coins around with their fingers.

Explore your neighborhood by having students locate local landmarks on a Mapquest map

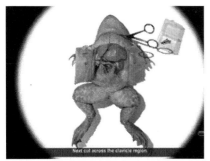

Create excitement in science with a simulated Froguts dissection.

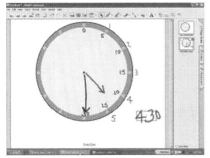

Build younger students' confidence in telling time.

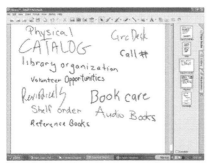

Lead the class in a creative writing brainstorming exercise.

Post a schedule of the week's assignments.

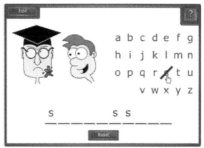

Use word guess to drill students on the week's basal words.

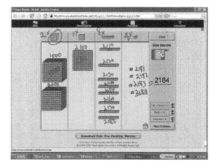

Interactively manipulate base ten blocks using the National Library of Virtual Manipulatives.

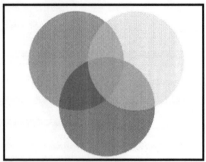

Experiment with color blending.

Learn about the lives of the U.S. Presidents.

Scan student work using a document camera, then use a SMART stylus to add information or make changes on the interactive whiteboard.

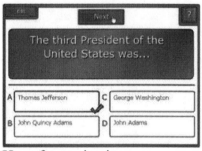

Have fun reviewing presidential facts with a quiz you create using the Lesson Activity Toolkit.

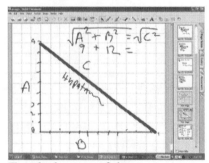

Teach the use of the Pythagorean theorem to determine the distance of the hypotenuse.

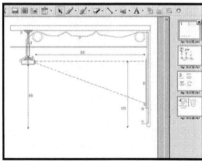

Create construction drawings in tech ed class.

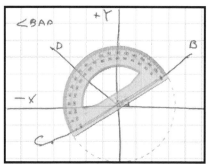

Teach geometric angles and protractor use.

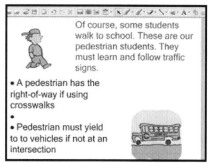

Make sure your students know bus safety rules.

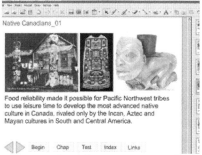

Access virtual museums and online collections to make history come alive.

Teach math students the basics of using their calculator.

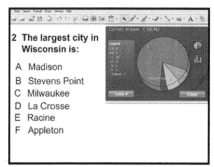

Use your SMART Board interactive whiteboard with a Senteo™ response system to simultaneously quiz all students in the class.

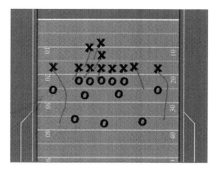

Diagram plays for the football team or other sport. Print out for team study.

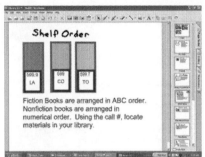

Teach the Dewey Decimal System and other library skills.

Import worksheets that students can write on. Students X'd things that cause erosion.

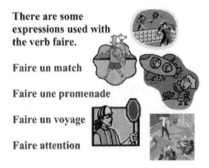

Use the interactive whiteboard for modern language instruction.

Explore plate tectonics using this Notebook file.

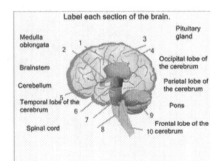

Have students label parts of the brain.

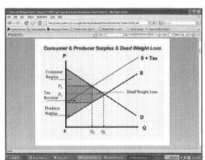

Post interactive whiteboard lecture notes to your web page for student review.

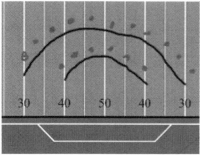

Diagram where the marching band will take the field.

Teach conducting to advanced music students using the SMART stylus as the baton.

You can do all of these things and more using Notebook software. Simple SMART Skills, Vol. 2, will help you learn all about Notebook software.

2

Welcome Center – an introduction

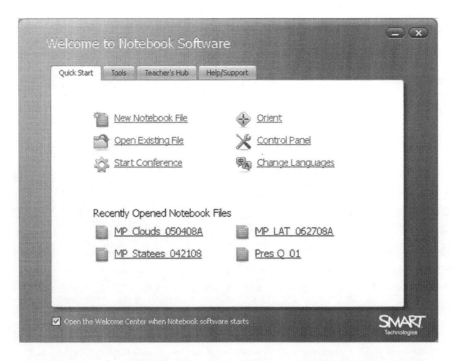

When you launch Notebook 10 software, the **Welcome Center** is the first new feature you see. The Welcome Center conveniently remembers the last four Notebook files you opened, so if you are teaching multiple sections of a class, or if a student closes Notebook, it is easy to get back to the Notebook files you were just using.

The Welcome Center allows you to customize Notebook software for your needs. For now, we will focus on just a few important items, and then get right into Notebook software.

Touch the **Quick Start** tab of the Welcome Center and you can create a **New Notebook File**, **Open Existing File**, go to **Recently Opened Notebook Files** or **Orient**. To orient an interactive whiteboard, aim a projector at the board, filling the screen as much as possible. After touching on these nine points, the software interprets your touch, sensing any coordinates.

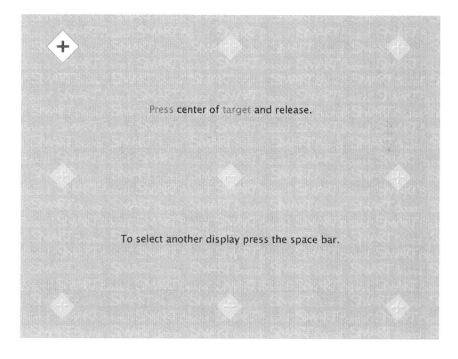

Press center of target and release.

To select another display press the space bar.

For great accuracy, use any of the stylus tips. Their smaller diameter makes orientation more accurate than using your fingertip. The point you lift up on is the orientation point.

Whenever you move the SMART Board or projector, you will have to reorient the board. If at any time you are pressing on the board with your finger or writing on it with a stylus, and feel the orientation is "drifting," just reorient the board.

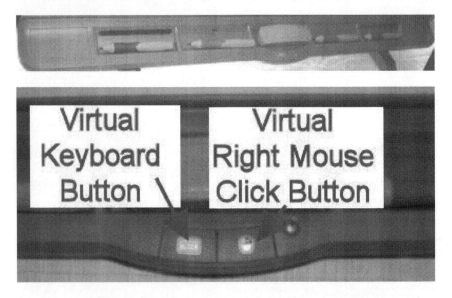

You can quickly reorient the board by simultaneously holding down the virtual keyboard button and virtual right mouse button on your SMART Board pen tray to call up the Orientation software.

Notebook 9 software did not have a Welcome Center screen. If you don't want the Welcome Center screen opening up whenever you use Notebook software, you can turn off that option by unchecking the box "Open the Welcome Center when Notebook software starts."

3

Thirtysomething tools

SMART Notebook software is a powerful tool to help you make classroom presentations engaging and interactive. We are going to explore the thirtysomething tools in SMART Notebook 10. We say "thirtysomething," because you can now customize the appearance of your toolbar (now up to 39 tools), depending on the simplicity or complexity you desire (a welcome feature missing since Notebook 8).

The Notebook software toolbar, along with the name of each commonly used tool, appears below and on the following pages:

A – Previous Page   D – Open Document

B – Next Page   E – Save Document

C – Add Page

F – Paste

G – Undo

H - Redo

I – Delete

J – Screen Shade

K – Full Screen View

L – Toggle Dual Page Mode

M – Screen Capture Tool

N – Document Camera Tool

O – Table Tool

P – Select Tool

Q – Pen Tool

R – Creative Pen Tool

S – Eraser Tool

T U V W X

T – Line Tool   W – Magic Pen Tool

U – Shapes Tool   X – Fill Tool

V – Shape Recognition Tool

Y Z AA

Y – Text Tool   AA – Toggle Toolbar

Z – Properties

To add or remove items from the toolbar, hold the right click key down on your Windows mouse (or use the "right-click" button on the SMART Board interactive whiteboard pen tray) and touch anywhere on the toolbar.

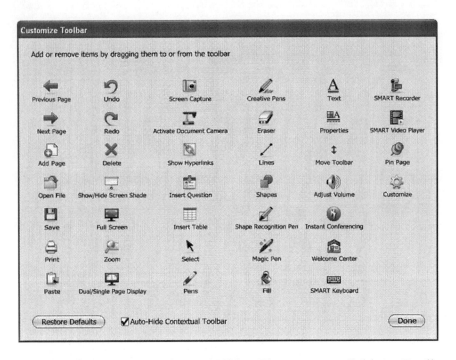

The SMART Recorder and Video Player are available as Toolbar icons only on the Windows version of Notebook 10, because these are Windows only features.

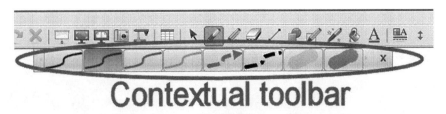

Contextual toolbar

Auto-Hide Contextual Toolbar (shown above at the bottom of the Customize Toolbar command box) is a new feature of the latest release of Notebook 10 software, letting you control Notebook software to hide the contextual menus (e.g. Pen, Line or Shape variants) when you touch in the Whiteboarding area of the Notebook page.

Pin Page, Zoom, and Customize have also been added since Notebook 10 was originally released.

For more help getting started using Notebook software, go to:
http://smarttech.com/trainingcenter/windows/trainingmaterials.asp
Click on Printed Windows Materials to see the Notebook 10 Toolbars
Quick Reference Guide on the tools and their functions.

We will now explore all the common Notebook tools, starting
from the left side of the toolbar.

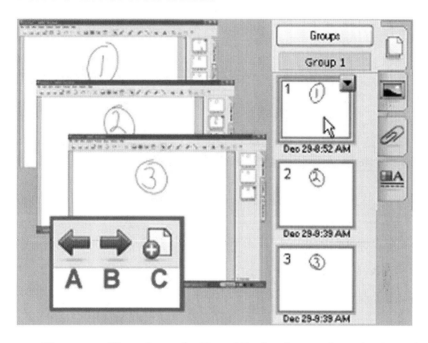

First we will see how the Page Navigation options (A,B, and C)
work. Start a new Notebook file by clicking on **Add Page** (C) twice to
create three time and date stamped Notebook pages (one page was
created just by starting a new Notebook file). You can navigate from
page to page by clicking on the thumbnails in the Page Sorter. You
can also navigate by clicking on **Previous Page** (A) or **Next Page** (B)
tools. Note the four tabs on the side: Page Sorter (highlighted in
blue), Gallery, Attachment and Properties.

Next, go to one of the Notebook pages you just created. Pick up a stylus from the pen tray and write on the interactive whiteboard. In the above example, we have written things we associate with cold weather. Click **Undo** (G) to undo your last action (in this example, the word "Mittens" in the upper right box). Click **Redo** (H) to bring back your last action.

Put the pens back in the pen tray and click on the object "Snow." Then click on the **Delete Tool** (I) to delete that object. The undo, redo and delete commands work with all objects, not just text, and are infinite, allowing you multiple opportunities to undo and redo.

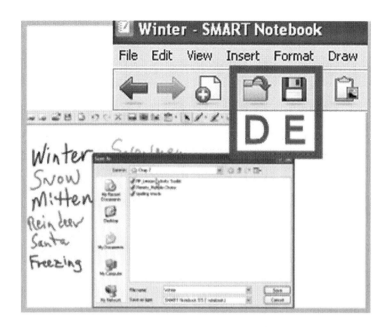

Click on the **Save** (E) tool to save your Notebook file. The Save
dialog box on your Windows will come up, and you can save like you
would save any other computer file.

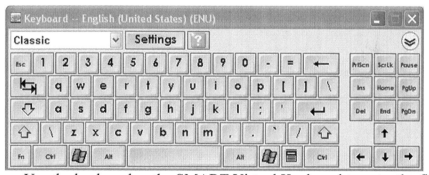

Use the keyboard or the SMART Virtual Keyboard to enter the file
name. Press on the pen tray's virtual keyboard key to access the
keyboard.

If you want to open up a previously saved Notebook file, click the
Open (D) tool. Your computer's Open dialog box pops up, letting you
navigate to where the file was saved and open it.

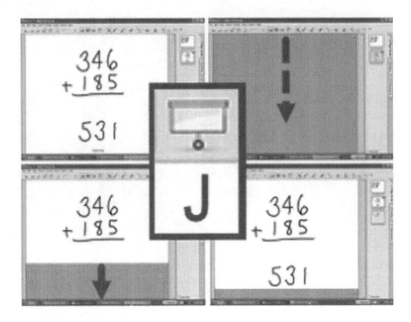

Now you will learn how to use the **Screen Shade** tool (J) to hide, then reveal, an answer. The Screen Shade is a modern version of the piece of paper used on an overhead transparency to reveal a problem or outline one step at a time. The image above shows the four steps of using the Screen Shade tool.

You can pull the Screen Shade from bottom to top, or from right to left, by grabbing one of the little "dimple" handles found at the center of each edge of the Screen Shade. To close the Screen Shade, click the red Close box on the upper right corner of the shade.

Now, position the Screen Shade in different locations on separate Notebook pages, then save your Notebook file. When you open it up again, the Screen Shades you created are where you set them, ready to use.

New in Notebook 10 is the ability to put Screen Shades in table cells.

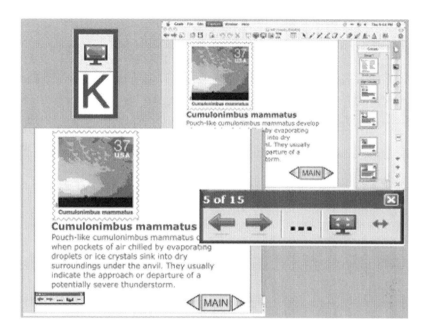

The **Full Screen View** tool (K) lets you hide distracting parts of Notebook and the bottom of your computer screen ("the Windows task bar"). Use the Full Screen View when you want to use Notebook for presentations or as a simple electronic whiteboard. In the illustration above, you see the "regular" mode (upper right), and the Full Page mode (lower left).

In the Full Screen View, a gray navigation bar pops up. Grab and drag the blue horizontal handle (in this example, the area which says "5 of 16") to move the navigation bar around the page. Use the Previous Page and Next Page arrows to move between Notebook pages. Click on the blue **Full Screen View toggle** icon (white triangles pointed inward) to return to the normal mode.

The Full Screen View enlarges Notebook pages about 25%, improving readability, especially for those students sitting at the back of the classroom.

In Notebook 10, the Full Screen Navigational Toolbar can be expanded by pressing on the black Expansion arrows on the right side of the toolbar. This gives you access to Add Page, Undo, Select, Magic Pen (nice for spotlighting, magnifying and annotating with fading ink), a pull down menu to access additional Notebook tools, and the Close Full Screen toggle. Here are the tools available via the More Tools (…) menu:

Insert Blank Page	Ctrl+M
Undo	Ctrl+Z
Redo	Ctrl+Y
Screen Shade	
Select	Ctrl+1
Magic Pen	Ctrl+9
Pen	Ctrl+2 ▶
Creative Pen	Ctrl+3 ▶
Eraser	Ctrl+4 ▶
Line	Ctrl+5 ▶
Shapes	Ctrl+6 ▶
Fill	Ctrl+7
Text	Ctrl+8 ▶
Magic Pen Tool	Ctrl+9

3 of 3

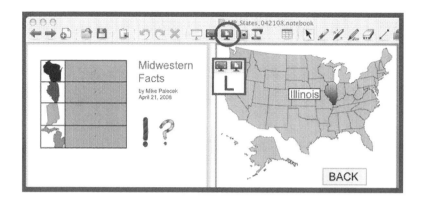

The **Toggle Dual Page Mode** (L) tool lets you compare two pages side by side. When you are in the two page mode, the icon turns into a single page icon, allowing you to toggle between the single page and dual page mode.

Some teachers create Notebook files as a "big book," and flip through pages so students can read the content as a group. When you touch the next or previous page arrows, the pages of the book "turn."

You can also anchor a page, using "Pin Page," fixing the page in place. In this example, we might pin the Midwestern Facts page and use it as a table of contents. Then, when students click on the pictures of Wisconsin, Illinois, Indiana and Michigan, the page at the right will change to show the state's location on the U.S. map. (Learn more about using Pin Page on page 83-84.)

You can also create objects on one page, and drag them to another page. An example would be having a home layout on one page. Then you could drag infinitely cloned furniture objects from the Gallery, onto the pinned page.

The next tool we will discuss is the **Screen Capture** tool (M). It can be accessed from Notebook software (as shown) or from the Floating Toolbar.

Using your finger as the mouse, click on the Capture (M) icon to bring up the Capture tool window. Press on one of the four capture icons: Area, Full Screen, Window or Freehand capture.

Above, we are doing an Area capture from a website on cloning. To capture an image into a Notebook page, follow these steps:

1. In Notebook, click on the Capture tool.

2. Go to the content you want to capture (the web page, etc.).

3. Click on one of the four capture icons in the Capture tool window.

4. Press one corner of the image you want to capture. With firm pressure, quickly drag to the opposite corner.

5. Remove your finger from the SMART Board interactive whiteboard.

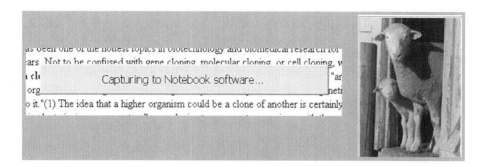

You will see the message "Capturing to Notebook software..." and your image will appear on the upper left corner of a new Notebook page. Here you see Dolly the cloned sheep, captured from a website.

The Screen Capture Tool works with virtually any software, not just websites. If, for example, you want to capture screen shots of your favorite mathematics simulation program, SMART's Screen Capture Tool is one way to do it.

Corel's Paint Shop Pro X is our favorite Windows screen capture tool. Paint Shop Pro lets us take timed screen shots with a 200 dots per inch resolution. Notebook Screen Capture is only 72 dots per inch. Paint Shop Pro X was used extensively for the graphics in this book.

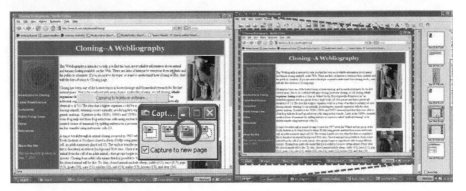

If, while you are doing an area capture, you hold down on the interactive board and don't drag your finger, the entire viewable page (full screen) will be captured. This is the same as selecting the Full Screen Capture tool. If you make a mistake and don't keep pressure on the interactive whiteboard while you are dragging, only a small cropped image will be captured.

The Full Screen Capture tool captures everything you see on your screen.

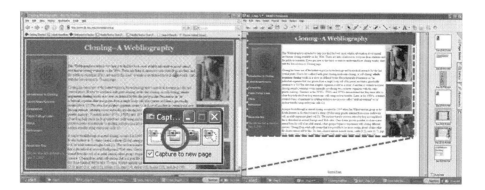

The next capture tool, Region Capture, captures a framed region. To see the different regions of the screen, click on this tool, then press on the interactive whiteboard. Continue to apply pressure while moving your finger around. In the example on the prior page, the website content is one frame, and the browser (above, with the URL address and menu commands) is in another frame.

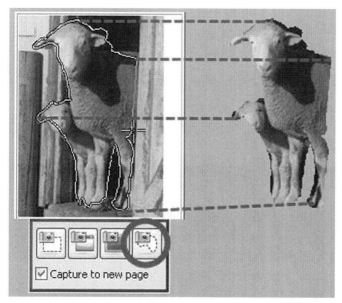

Although a little harder to use, the Freehand Capture tool adds great versatility in creating highly manipulative Notebook objects.

Touch the Freehand Capture tool once, then lift your hand off the interactive whiteboard. Press on one edge point of the image you want to capture. Firmly push and drag, tracing around the image. Freehand Capture works like the lasso tool found in drawing programs.

If you do not reconnect your beginning and end point, the tool will connect them with a straight line to finish off the irregular capture. Hint: if there is a straight line in the drawing, such as the frame of the barn door in the picture of Dolly, the cloned sheep, you might want to start your tracing at the spot where the back of the mama sheep is in contact with the door frame, trace around the image, and finish up where the belly is in contact with the door frame.

Lift off the interactive whiteboard to capture the area you defined.

The **Document Camera** tool (N) is a new feature of Notebook 10. You can place a 3-D object under the SMART SDC-280 document camera, and all your students can see it larger than life. Click on the Document Camera tool to bring up the live digitizing window. Here you can point out features and rotate the object.

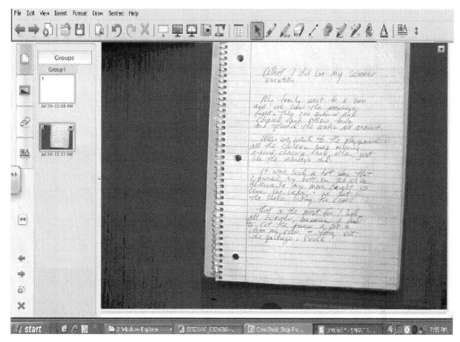

On the fly, you can collect student themes, choose one at random and put it down on the document base to digitize it. This helps students see the variety of different writing techniques, and allows for immediate class critiques.

You can also quickly capture maps, drawings, textbooks and newspaper images. You can digitize and/or present large scale objects, like maps and plans, capturing them into Notebook software and annotate over them, if desired. What a great way to make a "big book" out of EVERY book. Remember to keep copyright issues in mind.

An art teacher we know uses her document camera to teach art and art history. She buys "postcard art" at museum gift shops, because she cannot afford to buy full size prints and does not have room to store them. Using a document camera lets her display images in a large format, and lecture on artistic style and technique. Students can also make presentations on their own artwork.

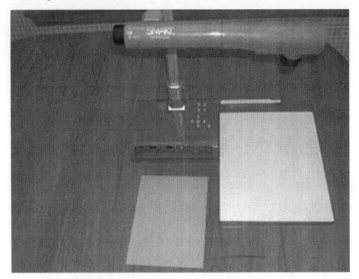

SMART Technologies' Document Camera (SDC-280) is the **ONLY** document camera that integrates directly with Notebook 10 software for Windows and Macintosh OS. The SDC-280 is 100% plug-and-play, so you can take it right out of the box, plug it in, and start using it without installing software other than Notebook 10 software on your computer. Because it takes only three seconds to digitize, you don't waste valuable instructional time.

Tables (O) is a new Notebook 10 feature. Return to page 21 and look at the Midwestern Facts table on the left side of the screen.

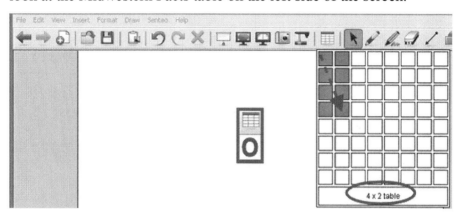

Touch the Tables icon and a grid appears. Touch on the upper left corner of the Tables grid. Push firmly and drag down to select the size table you want to create. In this example, we are creating a 4x2 table.

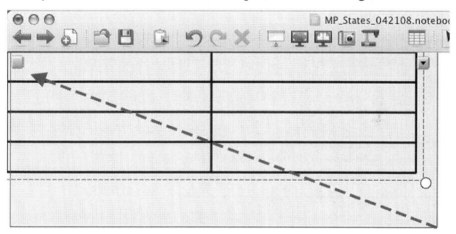

The table pops up in the upper left corner of the Notebook page, like any other pasted object. To select the table, get the Select tool and draw a marquee around the table (point your finger outside the table area, firmly press your finger down and drag to the upper left corner of the Notebook page). On the right side of the table, you will see the familiar Object Menu (triangle) and Resize handle (circle).

Touch the square Tables Drag handle on the upper left corner of the selected Table to drag the Table to the position you desire.

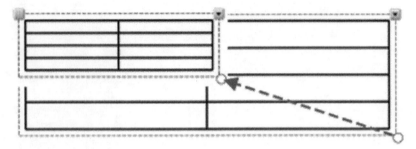

Touch the resize handle and drag it to create the desired table width (shown above).

In this example, we want the first column to eventually have square cells, about the size of a postage stamp, to drag and drop states from the Gallery. Using the Select tool, drag the table column divider to the left.

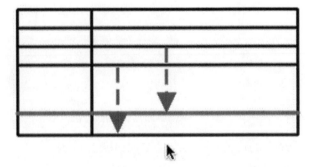

Pull down on the row dividers. First, point to the lowest row divider and drag it to the depth you want. This will create the black edged cell at the lower left of the image. Pull down on the next lowest row. If you pull down (keep your finger firm against the interactive whiteboard) and follow through (shown by the black pointer going beyond the table) the row you create will be the same height as the preceding row.

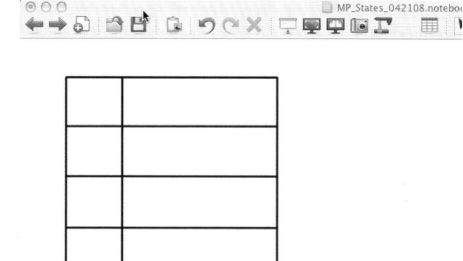

This is how your final table will look. You can now drag and drop any Notebook object into the table cells. One nice feature is that any graphics you drag into the table are instantly resized to properly fill the cell. Anything you can drag into Notebook from another program can be dropped into a cell.

Many of the new features of Notebook 10 are <u>not</u> "backwards compatible." If you are creating Notebook files to share with others, consider that they might still be using Notebook 9. Tables cannot be read by Notebook 9 and will appear as blank pages. To create a Notebook 9 version of a table created in Notebook 10 software, do a Screen "Area" Capture of the table. Then paste it as a new page, finishing off by adding objects, creating links, etc.

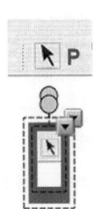

The **Select** tool (P) is constantly used to select and manipulate objects. It is also used when working with the Object Menu and the Notebook pull down menus. The SMART Board interactive whiteboard is in the Select mode, until you pick up a stylus or choose a software tool.

Hint: if you cannot seem to make things work correctly in Notebook, touch on the Select tool and then select the object or tool you want to use.

The **Delete** (I) and **Properties** (Z) tools only work when you have selected an object with the Select tool.

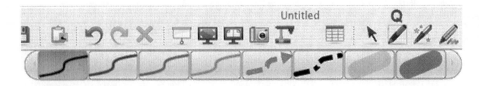

In addition to the four styluses in the pen tray, the **Pen** tool (Q) gives you six additional pens and two highlighters.

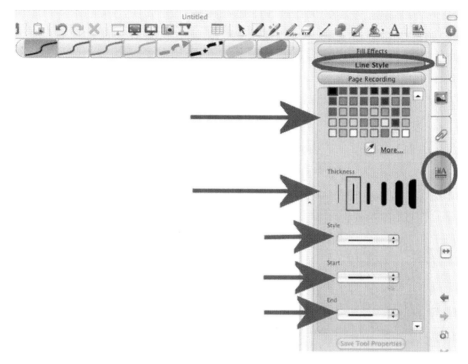

When a pen is selected using the onscreen pen tool, you can touch on the Properties Tab and select **Line Style** to change its properties, including color, thickness, line style, start and end points. Touch the **Save Tool Properties** button to save the properties of the selected pen. This does not affect the properties of the stylus pens in the Pen Tray, just the "virtual" pens in Notebook software.

Fill Effects lets you to further customize any of these pens and highlighters with varying degrees of translucency and an additional inner line color.

Hint: you may want to create a white pen so you can "write over" objects that are on a white background, then later erase the white ink to reveal information.

Everyone has fun with the **Creative Pen** (R). Touch and drag
down on the Creative Pen tool to choose the creative pen style you
want to use. You can write with it, or use it as a stamp, as we did
(above) in making periods. You cane even change the thickness of
creative pen lines.

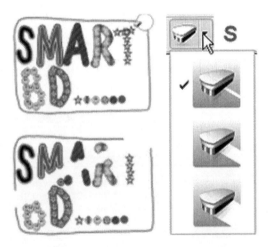

The **Eraser** (S) tool gives you three eraser widths, and works like
the eraser in the pen tray.

Using the Eraser, you can also erase a large area quickly by tracing a lasso around your drawing. You won't see the lasso… just imagine it. Make sure to connect the eraser's beginning and end point. Then, very quickly, lift up off the interactive whiteboard, and then touch (with the eraser still active) anywhere in the middle of the lasso.

Everything you lassoed will be erased. This is much faster than erasing everything, like you would if you were holding a real eraser and wiping the interactive whiteboard clean.

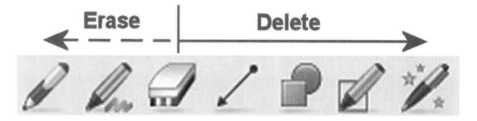

Objects created using drawing tools (to the LEFT of the eraser) can be erased. Objects using vector tools (to the RIGHT of the eraser) cannot be erased; they must be selected and deleted. An exception is that if objects were created using drawing tools and then grouped, this new group can be deleted, but not erased.

Think of a drawing tool as a set of dots grouped together in a line or curve. A vector tool has a beginning point and a geometric vector description to another point (i.e. rectangle).

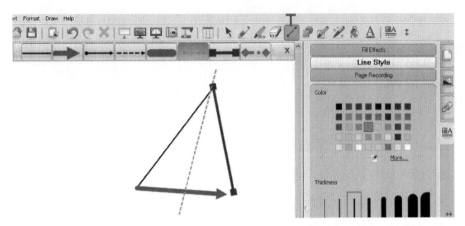

The **Line** tool (T) offers eight customizable lines, via a drop down contextual toolbar. Customize lines using Properties the same way you did with the Pens (Q) tools.

As vector-based objects, Lines can be moved by clicking on the Select (P) tool. Line thickness, color, end points, solidness and transparency can be changed via the Properties tool or tab. Lines cannot be erased, but they can be selected and deleted.

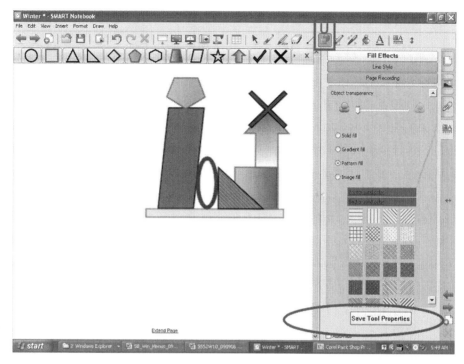

The **Shapes** (U) tool gives you 15 shapes via a drop down menu. Customize Shapes the same way you customize Pens (Q) and Lines (T).

The same rules that apply to Lines regarding moving, setting properties and selecting/deleting also apply to Shapes. On the right side of the screen, above, you see the Properties Tab Fill Effects menu. The rectangle object is set to solid (for zero Object transparency, the slider is all the way to the left). The Pattern Fill radio button was selected. The Foreground Colour (remember that SMART is a Canadian company) text is clicked to choose the color red, then the Pattern Fill radio button was selected again, to choose the left-to-right diagonal pattern.

Note that gradient and pattern shapes are new Notebook 10 features. If you are writing Notebook files that Notebook 9 users will run, use solid filled shapes only. Gradient and pattern shapes will appear as unfilled black and white shapes when a Notebook 10 file is opened by a Notebook 9 user.

Also note, if you use an Unfilled shape and select it, you can select, move it, or use it for a link, ONLY by touching the colored edge, not the unfilled center of the shape.

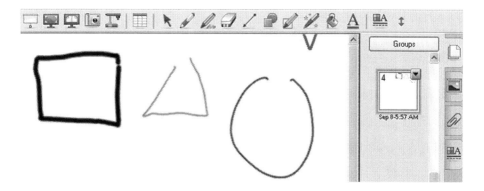

Using the **Shape Recognition** (W) tool, you can draw a freehand circle, oval, triangle, rectangle or square, and Notebook 10 will convert your rough shape into a vector graphic. The object does not have to be completely connected, as you can see from the triangle and oval shown above.

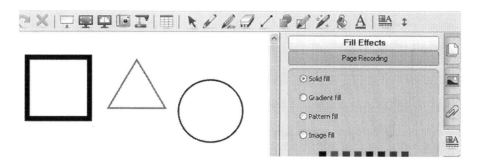

You can specify various properties, such as line thickness and color, as shown above.

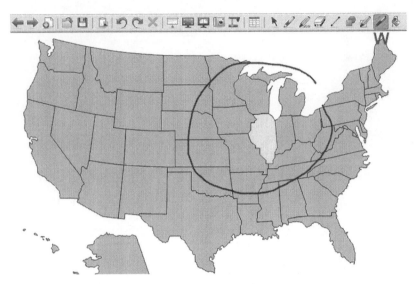

The **Magic Pen** (W) can be used in three ways: to draw an oval to create a Spotlight, to draw a rectangle to magnify, or to create fading lettering.

To make a Spotlight, you do not even have to complete the oval. The Magic Pen will complete the oval and turn it into a Spotlight.

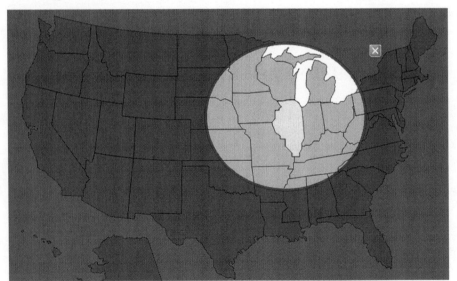

To go back to normal mode, touch the red close box.

To enter Notebook 10's new scalable Magnify mode, draw a rectangle with the Magic Pen. Tap your finger in the magnified section and drag in to zoom in (magnify less), pull out to zoom out. Touch on the red "X" close box to exit the Magnify mode.

In the Magnify mode, Notebook 10 puts a thin 3-D framework behind the image to reference the magnification amount.

When you write with the Magic Pen, after five seconds, the magic ink will start fading away. Use the Properties tool or tab to modify the magic ink color and thickness.

Used sparingly, the Magic Pen adds interest to your presentation. Like any magic trick, use it only occasionally, for special effect.

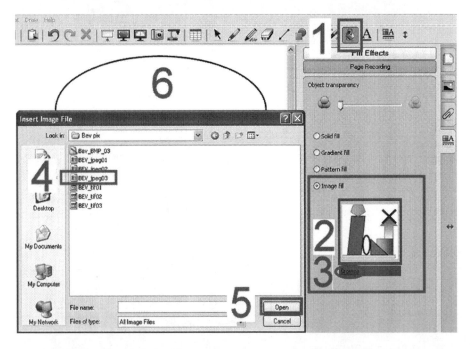

The **Fill** tool (Y) is another new feature of Notebook 10. Using the Shapes or Shape Recognition tools, you can create objects. Later, you can fill in these objects with the Fill tool. You can specify properties for the fill, including object transparency, solid fill (color), gradient fill (two colors and transition style), pattern fill (two colors and any one of 12 different patterns) or an image fill.

In the above illustration, we did an image fill. After drawing and selecting an oval, #1 – we selected the Fill tool. #2 - we touched the Image Fill radio button, #3 - touched the browse button to point to the file we wanted to use. Then, in #4 – we selected the desired file and #5 clicked the Open button. The Windows version of Notebook 10 software opens BMP, JPG, PNG and TIFF images. In #6 – our selected image was filled into the oval.

Ideally, the image should be about the same size as the object you are filling. If it is too big, you will fill from the upper left corner of the object. If it is too small, you will get multiple copies of the image.

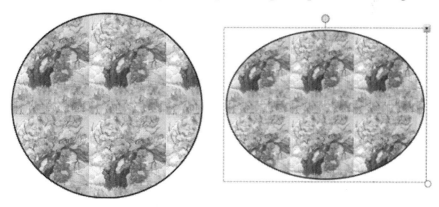

This painting of an oak tree was scanned in using the SMART Document Camera and resized using Paintshop Pro. In the image on the left, you can see what happened when the circle was filled by using Image Fill. Then, by using the Select tool, the image was resized by pulling on the resize handle on the lower right of the circle, reshaping the circle into an oval for a more symmetric "cameo" look.

To exit the Fill Tool, simply select another Notebook tool.

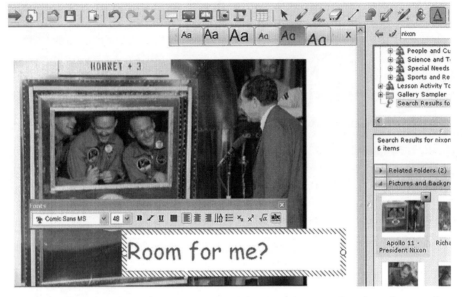

The **Text** tool (Y) has been a familiar tool in Notebook software for many years. In this Notebook Gallery file, President Nixon is joking with the Apollo 11 astronauts after their moon walk.

In Notebook, you see the text tool selected at the upper right corner of the Tool Bar. Six different default font/size/style choices are in the Contextual Toolbar (above Nixon's head). We touched on the SMART Board just below the astronauts, and typed in "Room for me?" Notebook's Text toolbar has popped up just above the text.

In Notebook 10, the "pull down" choices appear on a menu bar, which is horizontal instead of vertical. Font, size, style (bold, italic, underline), color, justification (left, center, right), bullets, subscript, superscript and math symbols (Special Characters), are all the same as in Notebook 9.7.

To use it, touch the Text tool, touch in the active whiteboarding area, and start typing with the computer keyboard or the SMART virtual keyboard. To make changes, highlight the text as you would in a word processor.

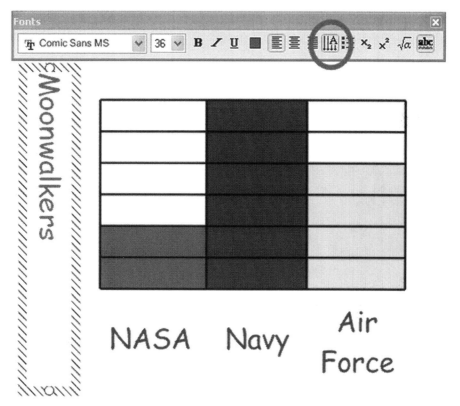

The Text Toolbar in the Windows version of SMART Notebook has a vertical text tool. In this example, we created a 6x3 table, resized the row widths, chose Properties, selected cells to highlight, and chose a solid color. Then, we chose the Text tool and then the Vertical tool, and typed in text for the side of the table.

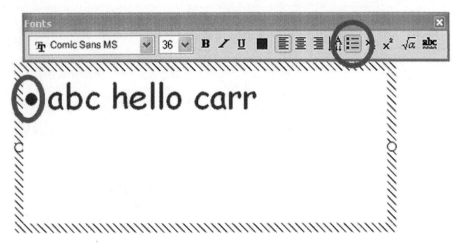

Click on the bullets tool to enter bullets in front of text.

When the bullets tool is active, press return and start typing again to create another bullet.

Doing a Subscript or Superscript is easy. Simply type out your text, highlight the text you want to superscript (in this example this algebra formula will be for $2b^2$). Then click the Superscript tile. (You can subscript H_2O as well).

Within the Text Tool is the Math Symbols tool. When you touch on the Math Symbols tool (looks like a square root), you can view different language symbols by clicking on the different Greek symbols in the lower section of the Text Tools box. These are the various available Math symbols:

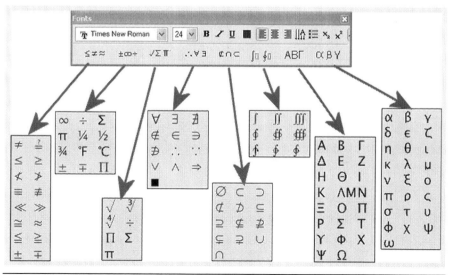

Touch the different Greek symbols to explore over one hundred different symbols that you can use as text in Notebook.

If you use Notebook software on both the Macintosh and Windows OS platform, you will find more symbols in the Macintosh OS.

We are often asked how to create fractions in Notebook software. The best way is with Fraction Maker from the Essentials for Educators' Gallery (see page 155).

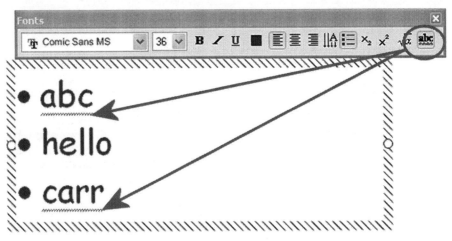

Text tool spell checking is a Windows Notebook 10 software feature. Click on the spelling tool to activate. When you type, text which is not in the dictionary is marked with a wavy red underline. You can also toggle the spell checker on and off, to check spelling in a text block.

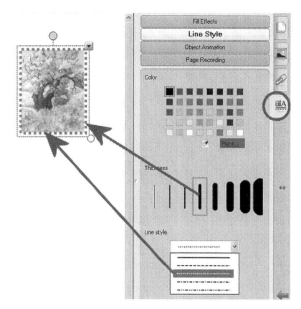

The different attributes of the **Properties** tool (Z) have been explained already. The Properties tool gives an additional dimension to each of the other Notebook tools. Above, we applied an exact line thickness and style to the outline of a filled shape.

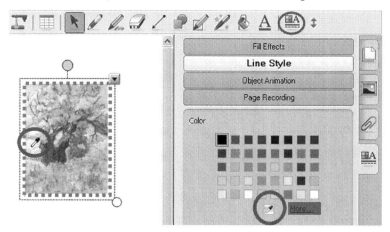

SMART Notebook's Properties Tool lets you pull a specify color from a graphic for a perfect match, as well as different line styles. Here, pick a particular color from an imported JPEG, to color match the dashed border. More Properties information on pages 160-173.

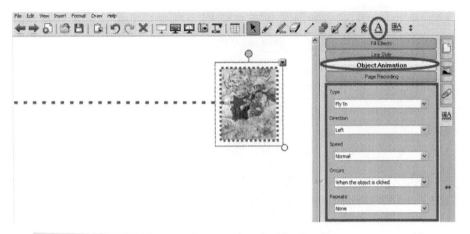

Object Animation is new in Notebook 10. It allows you to add simple object animation to your work. Making Object Animation work is simple. Just put the object where you want it in on the Notebook page, then touch Properties, the Object Animation sub tab, and use the pull down menus to select the animation attributes you desire for this object.

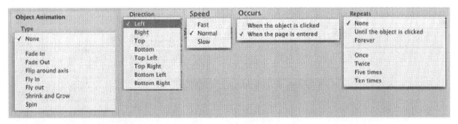

The above image shows all the different Object Animation attributes. Keep in mind that a Notebook 9 user will not see Object Animation. When played back on Notebook 9, the user only sees the final location of the object.

Our favorite animation is: <u>Type</u>: Fly In; <u>Direction</u>: Left; <u>Speed</u>: Normal; <u>Occurs</u>: When the page is entered; <u>Repeats</u>: None.

Another new Notebook 10 feature is **Page Recording**. Built into Notebook 10, Page Recording is much easier to use than SMART Recorder. To use it, touch Properties, Page Recording and the square icon recorder. A red REC(ord) button pops up on the upper left corner of your Notebook page. Then just do your work on Notebook and your actions are recorded. Touch the square button to stop recording.

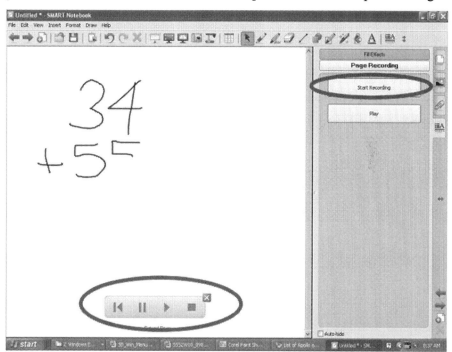

A playback bar then appears at the bottom of the page. Click the Play icon to replay your work, and the rewind, still or stop buttons as needed.

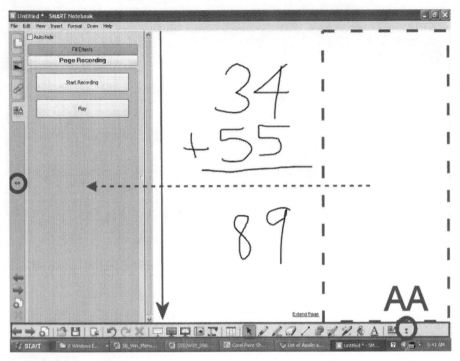

Use the **Toggle Toolbar** (AA) to move the Notebook Toolbar from the top of the screen to the bottom. This makes it easier for shorter people to reach Notebook Tools.

There is also a toggle for the Tabs area of Notebook, shown by the square with two arrows inside, to move the tabs area from the left to the right side of the Notebook page.

The toggles were available in earlier versions of Notebook, but look slightly different.

4

Notebook™ Menus

The real power of Notebook software is found in its pull down menus and object menus. Once you master these aspects of Notebook, you will find that it is a true authoring program, reminiscent of programs like Apple Computer's HyperCard and Roger Wagner's Hyperstudio. Notebook software does not handle variables, have an "authoring level," scripting, or send ASCII code to external devices, but you can do a tremendous amount of creative curricular software writing with Notebook.

The tasks done via pull down menus include managing Notebook files, manipulating objects, inputting, outputting, multimedia handling and many other tasks. Instead of skipping around and discussing each of these topics independently, this chapter will cover them as they appear as pull down menus, moving from left to right.

File Menu

We will cover the File menu commands of SMART Notebook 10 software in order to help you understand the full power of Notebook.

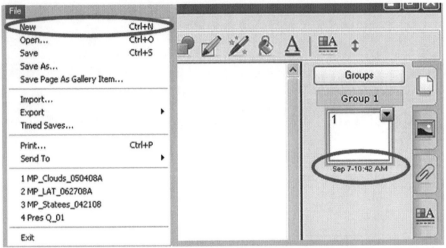

A **New** (Untitled) Notebook file is created. There is only one page in the Page Sorter. As each page is created, it is given a time and date stamp.

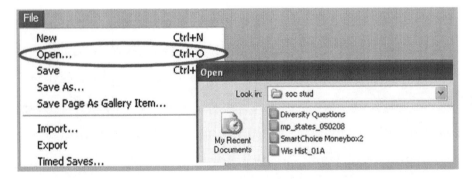

Open an existing Notebook file. This is a standard open dialog box for your Windows operating system. You can navigate to any storage device to find and open a saved Notebook file.

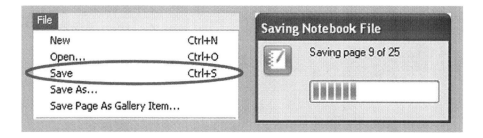

Save changes you made to a SMART Notebook file. **Save As...**
lets you rename the file and navigate to where you wish to save...

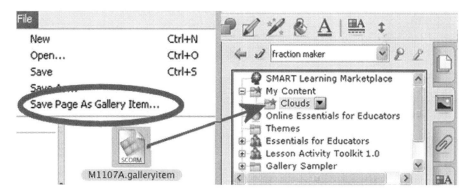

When you **Save Page as Gallery Item...** the entire Notebook page
you are viewing is turned into a Gallery Item. From the Windows
desktop, you see the SCORM Icon for the Gallery Item at the left
(M1107A.galleryitem). Drag and drop the SCORM item into the My
Content to use it in all Notebook files.

If you save this SCORM file to your desktop, and you double click
on the SCORM file, a new Notebook opens up using this Gallery Item
page as the background.

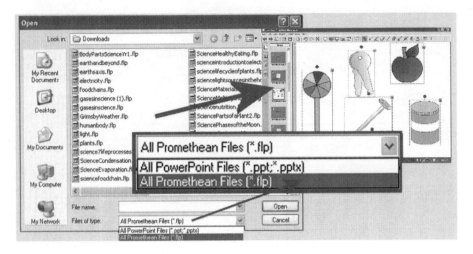

File->**Import** command is a Windows only Notebook software feature. It lets you convert Microsoft PowerPoint™ (PPT) and Promethean™ Flipchart (FLP) files to Notebook files.

Because Notebook software is a great presentation and content creation tool, why not import a PPT or FLP, show it in a class, then use the familiar Notebook software interface to make changes and resave it as a Notebook file. If you had some colleagues who (oops) bought a Promethean interactive whiteboard and were developing content, Notebook's Import command allows you to share content.

Many textbooks include teacher resource CDs, filled with PowerPoint presentations. Import into Notebook software lets you make changes to these presentations, create hyperlinks and add document (worksheet) attachments.

Import is not perfect. We downloaded Promethean ActivStudio flipcharts from www.tlfe.org.uk/promethean/flipcharts. During conversion, one of the flipcharts built Notebook pages and titled them, but there were not any images.

Converting additional Flipchart files, we found that objects converted nicely, but grouping and links did not work. Still, you can run the Flipchart file and always group or lock objects and create links at a later time in Notebook software.

PowerPoint files import better. All PowerPoint transitions are lost, so each slide is shown it its final state, with links to other slides and websites intact. The build effects, such as flying text points, are skipped. After sitting through a lot of lengthy PowerPoint presentations, we think that maybe that is a good thing.

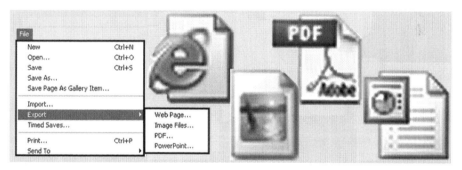

You can **Export** from Notebook to many different file types. The Windows version can also export to PowerPoint.

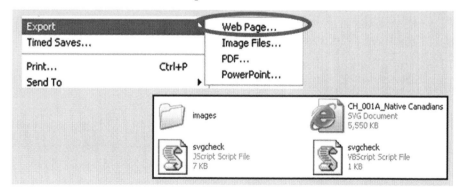

When you export as **Web Page**, Notebook software builds a navigation "skin" around your HTML package. You can then upload the HTML package (see the illustration above) to your learning management system website. This export is very quick and easy to do.

Any links you created in Notebook software will still work in the HTML package. Double click on the html file. Your browser opens up and the SVG (Scalable Vector Graphics) file is displayed in a browser window. Keep all of the created content in the same folder.

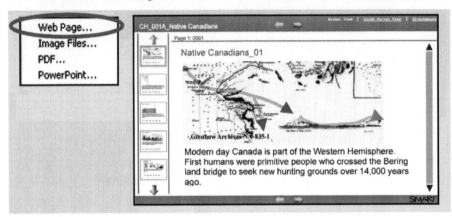

Here we see an exported Notebook file "Native Canadians_01" being displayed by the Safari browser. Web browsers are increasingly able to play back SVG files. You can find SVG plug-ins for different browsers at www.adobe.com/svg/viewer/install

A student using an older computer, accessing an exported Notebook file via the internet, may need to install a plug-in on their computer. At this Adobe website, you simply scroll down to find the operating system you are using, click the link, and a plug in application downloads to your computer. Double click on it, follow the installation instructions, and restart your computer.

Gee, that sounds complicated! Why do it? Exporting to web pages lets you post a Notebook 10 file online, so students can navigate through it, yet NOT change it. It is interactive, they don't need

Notebook software, all the links remain, and they can display Notebook 10 features.

On the upper right corner of the SVG skin, there are three commands: Normal View, Slide Sorter View and Attachments. Here we see the Slide Sorter View. Click on any of the slides to navigate to that slide.

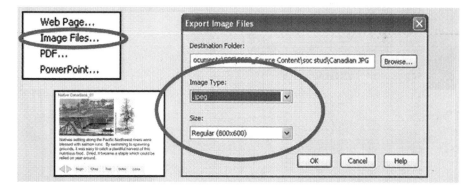

When you **Export Image File,** individual pages in Notebook software are converted and saved as graphics. These can easily be used in other software programs. Format options are JPEG (Joint

Photographic Experts Group), PNG (Portable Network Graphic), GIF (CompuServe Graphics Interchange) or BMP (Bit Map Picture).

If you want to use Notebook full screen shots in some other program (PowerPoint, Word, Dreamweaver, Front Page, etc.) use Export Image File to convert the pages to images.

You can save in different sizes - Tiny (200x150 pixel) thumbnails, Small (400x300), Regular (800x600) or Large (1024x768). If you are looking for a moderately good quality image with small file size, JPEGs are universally read by other software programs. A "Small" image is about the area of a quarter of your computer screen. An image can be further resized in many other computer programs, making it easy to size images to fit in your layout.

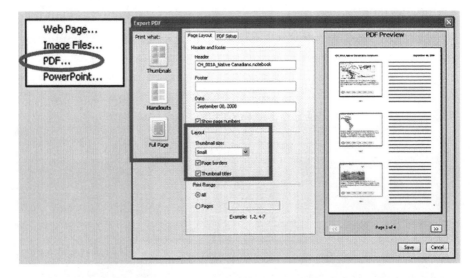

When you Export a file as a PDF, you quickly create a Portable Document File format which can be read with the free Adobe Acrobat Reader. We think of PDF as the "Rosetta Stone" of computer documentation. It's on virtually everyone's computer!

Export a PDF so you can email your Notebook lecture or post it to a web site. Click on the PDF style you want (in our case, Handouts) on the left side of this message box, and pull down to thumbnail size (medium) and a page of your PDF file will be displayed at the right. From a sixteen page Notebook file, you will create a six page PDF in under twenty seconds.

If you are using a Notebook file for a presentation, creating a PDF is a great way to print out handouts for your participants to use for their own note taking. It is also another way to put your class lecture notes on the Internet, or email them to students who have missed the lecture.

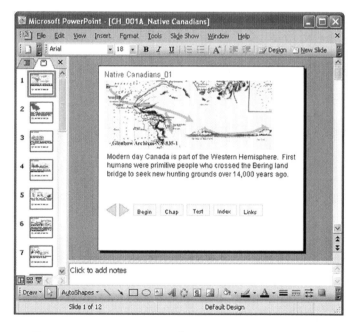

You can **Export to PowerPoint** in the Windows version of Notebook 10 software. Your links will stay active. Converted text can be edited in PowerPoint.

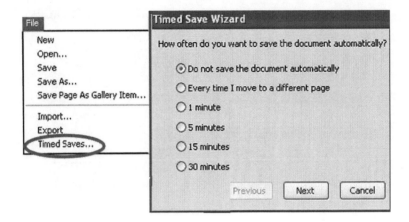

Some users want software that saves automatically, so they won't lose their work. Notebook 10 software for Windows can do **Timed Saves**. With the Timed Save Wizard you can choose how often you want your work saved, and file format (HTML web pages, PDF, time stamped PDF, image files, Power Point, or Notebook document.)

The **Print** window consists of three parts:

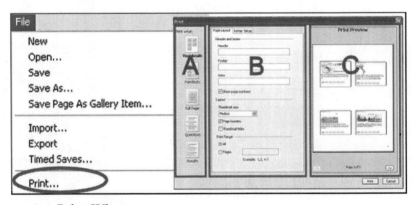

A – Print What

B – Page Setup

C – Print Preview

Thumbnails Handouts Full Page Questions Results

(A) Print What – gives you a choice of Thumbnails, Handouts and Full Page formats. Questions and Results formats only appears if you have the Senteo™ student response software installed.

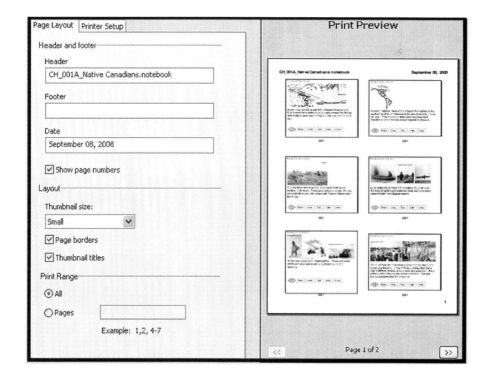

(B) Page Setup is slightly different depending on what type of notes you choose to print. Handouts are usually the most useful, because they include lots of room for notes. In Handouts, you can select Large (1 per page) Thumbnails, Medium (2 per page) or Small (3 per page).

Unless there is a lot of detail on a page, select Small. If you want more readability, select a larger size.

(C) Print Preview – You get to preview what your document will look like before you print it. When you click the Continue button, you get the standard Windows printer screen, allowing you to select your printer, page size, number of copies, page range, and preview features.

Sample print layout options include:

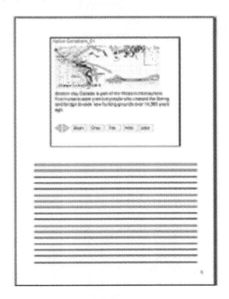

Handouts / large / portrait. Printed on an 8-1/2 x 11 sheet of paper, these options give you a very readable screen shot of each SMART Notebook page.

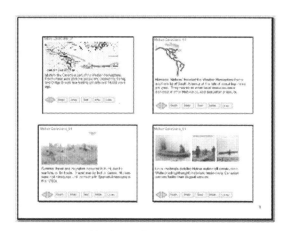

Thumbnails / medium / landscape. This is a good option if you don't need room for note taking. On an 8-1/2 x 11 sheet of paper, it also gives you a very readable screen shot of each Notebook page. It uses only 25% of the paper used in handouts / large / portrait.

SMART Notebook Print Capture

Only available in Notebook software for Windows, SMART Notebook Print Capture lets you print from any application into SMART Notebook. This is very similar to doing a Camera Capture, because the final Notebook object is a bit map image.

It is different, because a word processing file, for example, which is more than one screen high can be quickly captured onto into Notebook.

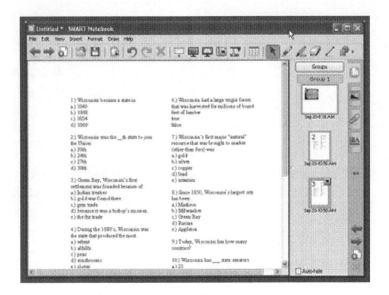

We took a two column Microsoft Word document and used Print to Notebook Software to bring the document into a Notebook page. The image is a little fuzzy, even at 300x300 resolution.

If a teacher wants to edit or manipulate text, it is better to highlight content in the word processor then copy and paste into Notebook software, or to use Microsoft Word and SMART's Ink Aware capabilities (page 183-186).

Try experimenting with printing websites to Notebook with the Print to Notebook Command.

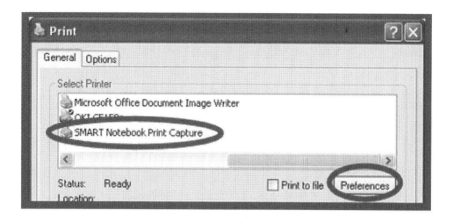

In the Windows print dialog box, select SMART Notebook Print
Capture, and then click on the Preferences button.

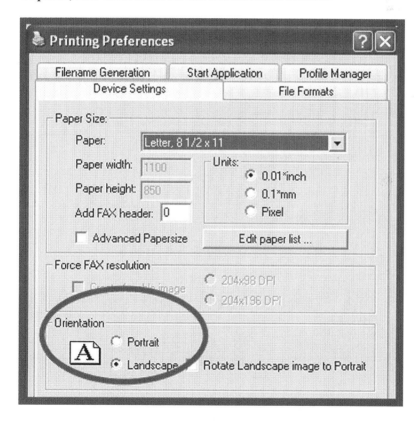

For best results with websites, change Orientation to Landscape.

Send To lets you email a Notebook file or PDF to anyone you have created an email profile for in the Microsoft operating system. You do this through the Mail feature in the Control Panel. Most users simply save their Notebook files or Export to PDF, then email their work.

The four **most recent** opened Notebook files are listed so you can easily go back and reopen them.

Exit allows you to exit from Notebook software.

Edit Menu

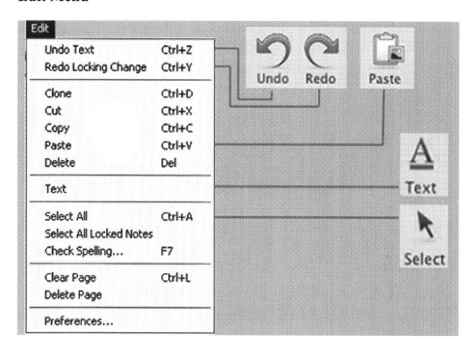

The **Edit** menu lets you do the typical things you would expect to do at an Edit menu - cut, copy, paste, undo and redo - as well as special SMART Notebook software features. You have already learned about many Edit Menu commands: Undo (page 16), Redo (page 16), Paste (page 12), Delete (page 16), Text (page 44), and Select (page 32).

When you create an object, **Undo** is highlighted. The Undo icon (counterclockwise curved arrow) also becomes blue. The type of object is identified after Undo. When you pull down to Edit/Undo, or click the Undo button, the last event you performed in Notebook software is reversed.

Redo becomes active when you Undo. The object type is identified in the pull down menu. The blue Redo icon (right curved arrow) also becomes active in the SMART Board tools strip.

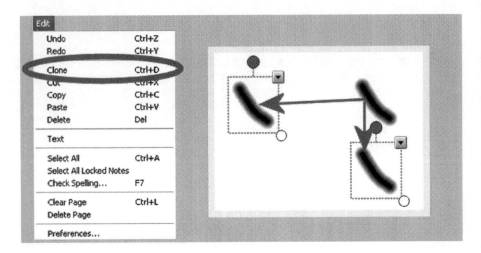

Clone is the same thing as performing a Copy and Paste. It is just a faster way to duplicate any Notebook object. To Clone, first Select the object you want to clone by touching it with the Select tool (the pointer arrow). Then select Clone. You can also Clone via the Object Menu, which is described on page 126.

Cut, **Copy**, **Paste** and **Delete** all work as you would expect. Select the object, then choose the command you wish to use. You can also use the familiar Control-X, C, and V keystroke shortcuts.

Selecting **Text** is like using the Text Tool (page 44) in Notebook. It can also be accessed from the edit menu, but it seems more intuitive to use the Text Tool.

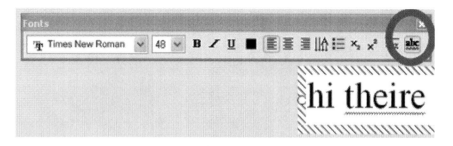

Spelling has changed in Notebook 10 software. In the Macintosh version, there is a "Check Spelling as You Type" in the Edit pull down menu. On Windows PCs, you access this feature through the Text Toolbar. Click on the "ABC" icon, and a dotted red line appears under the misspelled text.

If you "Check Spelling" from the Edit menu, a Spelling Dictionary pops up to help you properly spell any misspelled words. As with any dictionary, you can add new words by clicking on the "Add to Dictionary" button.

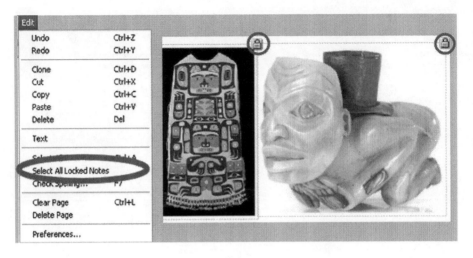

As you would expect, **Select All** selects all unlocked objects in Notebook software. **Select All Locked Notes** selects Notebook objects you have locked. Typically, you lock objects using the Objects Menu (page 127) to prevent others from deleting, rotating or moving objects in Notebook files you create.

If you want to make major modifications to a Notebook file, you can Select All Locked Notes, one page at a time, to unlock those objects on the page. You then pull down on any of the Lock symbols, and drag to Unlock. Then ALL of the objects on the page are unlocked.

In Simple SMART Skills: Volume 1, you learned how to go to SMART's Education website to download pre-built Notebook files. If you want to modify locked items on a page in a Notebook file you downloaded, the fastest method is to Select All Locked Notes and unlock these objects.

Clear Page erases all unlocked objects on a page and **Delete Page** deletes the page you are on from your Notebook file. These commands are more often invoked in the Page Sorter tab. Just click on a page thumbnail and access Clear Page or Delete Page from the Objects Menu for that page (page 136).

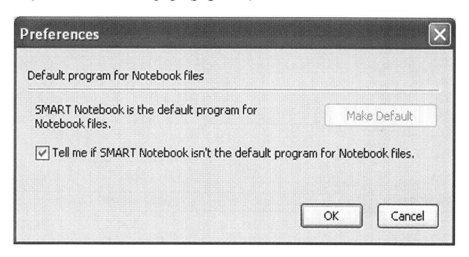

Preferences allow you set SMART Notebook software as the default program for reading SMART Notebook files. In Fall 2008, this became a brand new feature, with the introduction of the Beta release of SMART Notebook Student Edition

View Menu

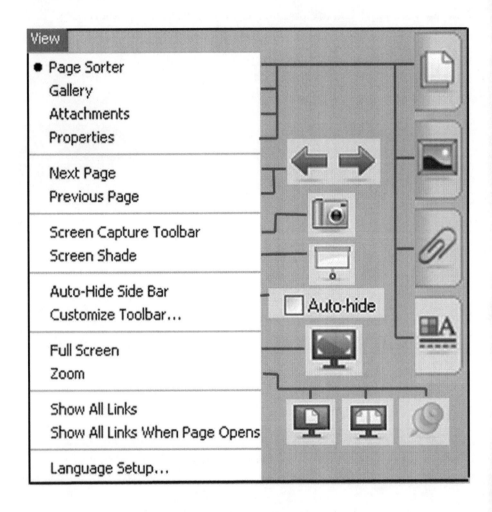

In **View**, you can view and access different Special "tab" Areas of Notebook: **Page Sorter** (page 135-139), **Gallery** (page 146-156), **Attachments** (page 157-159) and **Properties** (page 160-173). If you have install Senteo™ 2.0 software, you will see a Senteo tab.

You can navigate through your Notebook file by using the **Next Page** (page 15) and **Previous Page** (page 15) pull down commands.

You can use the **Screen Capture Toolbar** (page 22-26) and operate the **Screen Shade** (page 18).

You can use **Full Screen** (page 19-20) to hide Notebook tools and pull down menus, zoom in and out, and see links you have created. You can toggle to the **Dual Page Mode** (page 21) or back to the **Single Page Mode** (page 21), and **Pin Page** (page 83-84).

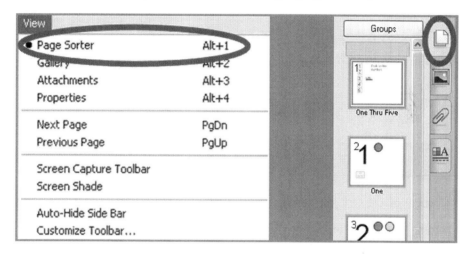

One way to access the **Page Sorter** is to point to View and pull down to select Page Sorter. However, most Notebook software users will click on the Page Sorter tab.

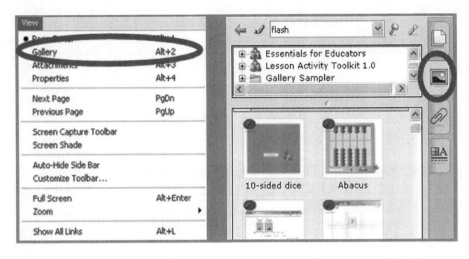

You can access the **Gallery** by pointing to View and pulling down to select Gallery or by touching on the Gallery tab. The Gallery is extensively covered on pages 146-156.

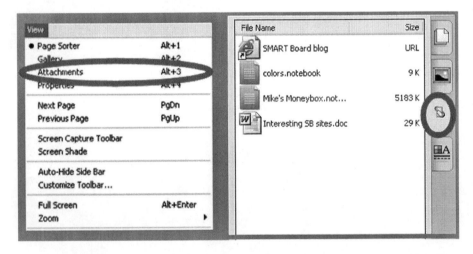

In **Attachments** you can store files for use with your Notebook file. Think of these as attachments to an email. If you have added attachments to your Notebook file and want to email them to others, or use the attachments from year to year, you can. These attachments are imbedded in your Notebook file, making them easy to find and share.

Here we see two Notebook files, a URL and an imbedded word document. To use them, drag the attachments to the Whiteboarding area of Notebook software, in this case as graphics or links, or double click on the attachments to launch the files. See pages 157-159 for more information on attachments.

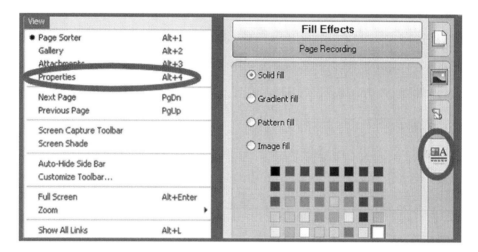

The **Properties** tab is a brand new Notebook 10 feature. You can also select an object and access the object Properties via the Properties Tool at the top of the Notebook screen (page 49-50). Another way to access Properties is via the Object Menu (pages 131).

Different objects have different properties. Most of them have transparency levels and fill effects. See pages 160-173 for more on Properties.

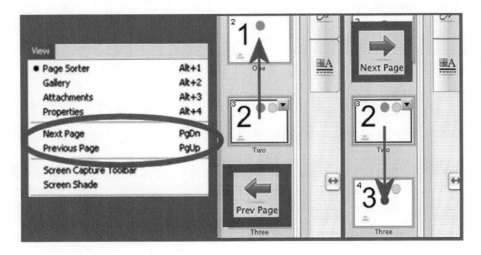

Previous Page lets you go back a page in Notebook software.

Next Page lets you navigate to the next page in a Notebook file. You can also do this by clicking on the next (or previous) page in the Page Sorter or by clicking on the Next (or Previous) Page Tool icon.

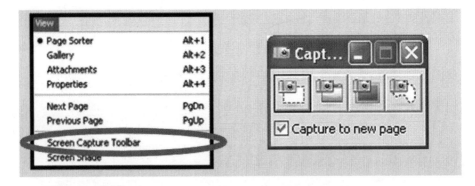

Screen Capture (pages 22-26) gives you four different methods to capture images and bring them into Notebook software. Click the Capture to New Page checkbox if you want Notebook software to open a new page every time you capture an image. If you do not have this checked and perform multiple captures, your images will all paste on top of each other in the upper left corner of the active Notebook page.

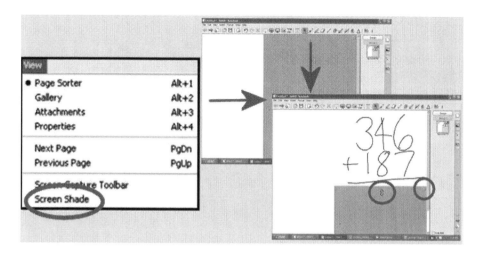

Screen Shade works like a piece of paper on top of an overhead transparency. Pull one of the dimpled handles to begin revealing a Notebook page. You can move the screen shade both horizontally and vertically, but two corners of the screen shade must touch the edges of a Notebook page. The Screen Shade is also accessed through the Tools menu and the Floating Toolbar.

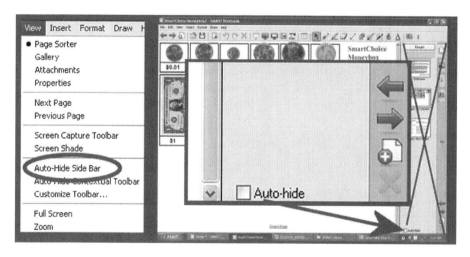

Auto-Hide Side Bar hides the side bar, which is the area shown when you click on the Page Sorter, Gallery, Attachments or Properties tabs. There is an auto-hide check box at the bottom of the side bar.

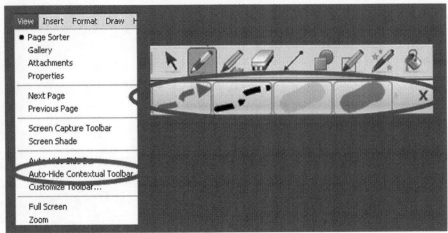

Auto-Hide Contextual Toolbar is a new Notebook 10 software feature. When you pick a virtual pen, you normally see eight different pens to choose from. This "contextual toolbar" of pen (or line, style, or text) choices is hidden, when you select Auto-Hide Contextual Toolbar, and after pressing the pen tool (and choices) press on the Whiteboarding area of Notebook software.

Customize Toolbar is the menu shortcut of right clicking on the Tools area of the Toolbar. You can then customize exactly which tools you want to use for your Notebook file, making the Notebook interface easier for younger or less experienced users. See pages 121-122 for more information on customizing the toolbar.

Full Screen gives you a Notebook software presentation without menus, tools or the special side tabs area. The images are bigger, so they can be seen better from the back of the classroom, and there are no distractors.

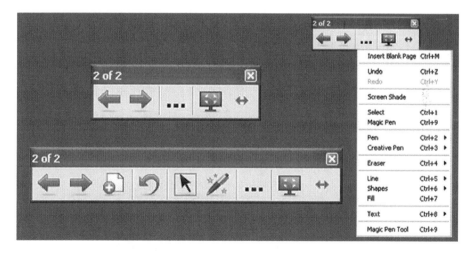

In the Full Screen mode, you get the navitagional tool bar (shown above, upper left), with tool icons for **Previous Page**, **Next Page**, **More Options**, and **Exit Full Screen**. You can drag the navigational tool bar around the screen by clicking and dragging on the blue header. Clicking the Exit Full Screen icon to go back to the previous view.

On the lower left of the screen above, we see the expanded Full Screen navigational toolbar of Notebook 10, with **Add Page, Undo** and **Select** tools, as well as the new **Magic Pen** Tool.

To access the **More Options** pull down menu as shown on the right side the prior figure, <u>touch and hold on the ... symbol</u>. Details about these tools are on pages 11-51.

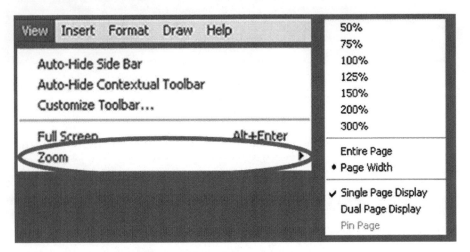

Zoom lets you view the page at different magnification levels. See a very long page with **Entire Page**. Normally, you will view Notebook files in a Single Page Display mode.

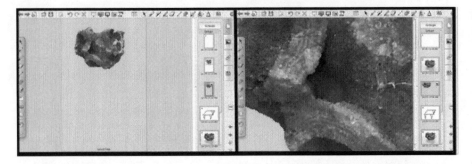

Usually you'd view your page at 100%, but if you want to point out additional visual detail to your class, you can use the zoom feature.

The Notebook file on the prior page shows a geode previously scanned into Notebook software using the SMART Document Camera and zoomed from 50% (at left) to 300% (at right).

Notebook software allows you to scroll around on a zoomed image. You can scan 3-D objects. Save your Notebook files and use them in class, zooming in to explore your images.

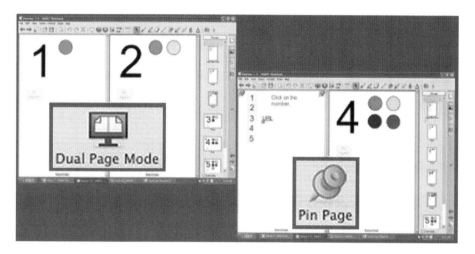

Zoom's **Dual Page Mode**, shown above, left, lets you look at two pages of <u>one</u> Notebook file side by side. On the left side we see two simultaneous Notebook pages, displayed like a "big book." Note the red rectangle around the right page, showing that it is the active page.

When selecting Dual Page Mode on the first page of a Notebook file, the page is displayed on the right side of the screen, with a blank area at the left side of the screen. Click the Next Page icon to move the page, and make it appear in the "book" format.

Pin Page after you select Dual Page Display to anchor (pin) a particular page into place. We pinned the Main page, so we can click on the yellow number squares in the table of contents, and see whatever page we select at the right. On the Main page (left side of right illustration) we clicked on the "4 box" to display Page Four (at right).

As noted above, when you first select Pin Page, Notebook software displays the pinned page on the right side, with the left side of the screen as blank. Use the Next Page tool to move the pinned page to the left side, then click on links on the pinned page to display the linked page on the right side of the screen.

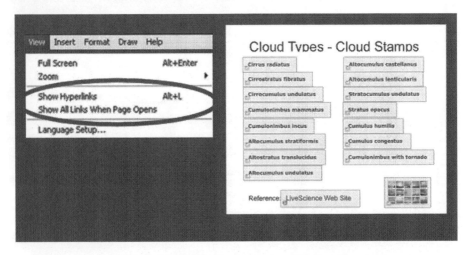

Show All Links flashes an animated green box around any link imbedded on the active SMART Notebook page. This can link you to a page in the file (page), website (globe), attachment (paper clip) or sound (speaker).

Show All Links When Page Opens lets you view the links when the page opens, instead of you "forcing" the viewing. We added the question mark on this picture to point out where one of the links appears to be missing. Using this command is a great way to quickly check your Notebook file for missing links.

Language Setup lets you change which language Notebook 10 software appears in. Modern language teachers will really love this Windows OS feature, because they can instantly change Notebook software over to 40 different languages. The top pull down lets you select which SMART applications (currently Notebook or SMART Board drivers software) to convert to a foreign language.

Bahasa Malaysia	Português (Brasil)
català	● português (Portugal)
Cymraeg	română
dansk	slovenski
● Deutsch	suomi
eesti	svenska
● English (United Kingdom)	Türkçe
● English	íslenska
● español (España)	čeština
Español (México)	ελληνικά
euskara	русский
● français	україньска
Gaeilge	Қазақ
galego	עברית
Gàidhlig	العربية
● italiano	हिंदी
Kiswahili	● 中文(简体)
lietuvių	● 中文(繁體)
Magyar	● 日本語
● Nederlands	● 한국어
norsk (bokmål)	
polski	

Above are all the display languages which you can display. Handwriting recognition closest match has a red dot in front of it.

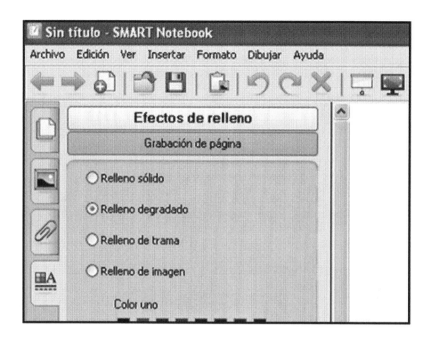

Notebook software looks like this when the Language Setup is changed to Spanish (España).

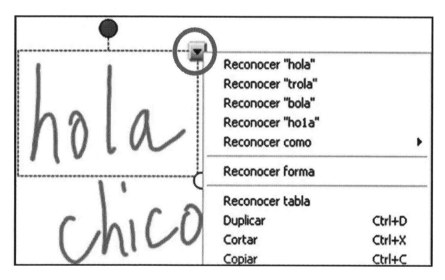

Touch the object pull down menu for handwriting recognition (page 124) for Spanish. In English, it is "hi boy."

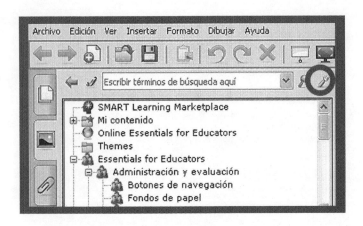

To list Gallery items in a foreign language, you have to click on the **Show All Gallery Actions** wrench tool and update the Essentials for Educators Gallery via the Internet.

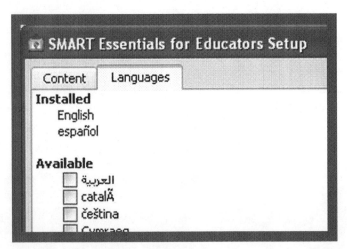

Click on the **Languages** tab and choose the additional Gallery language content you wish to install. You can also create your own Gallery items by dragging images to the "My Content" folder and put in foreign keywords. The virtual keyboard does not have accents, so you have to use alternate methods of entry. A great website on foreign language keyboard entry is:

http://www.starr.net/is/type/kbh.html

Insert Menu

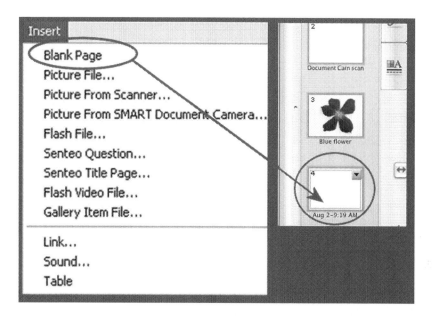

Blank Page inserts a new blank page in a Notebook file. It is inserted following the currently active page.

Above, we inserted an image of a U.S. postage stamp image taken from the internet. We used the **Picture File** command. The Insert Picture File command always inserts the picture at the top left corner of a Notebook page. To move it, just select the object with the Select ("pointer") tool or touch on it with your finger to drag it any location on the Notebook page, or drag it onto another Notebook page.

Insert **Picture from Scanner** lets you interact with your scanner's software through Notebook. If you have installed a scanner on your Windows computer, and the scanner has Twain-compliant drivers, your scanner software opens up. Use that software to control your scanner's contrast level, brightness, dots per inch density, color saturation and file format to save to. Save your scanned work, then open it up with the import picture command.

It is easy to Insert **Picture from SMART Document Camera**. This hanging blue clematis was picked from our backyard flower bed and scanned with a SMART Document Camera. To zoom in or out, use the zoom (magnify) + and – buttons on the left side of the scanning window that pops up in Notebook software. Then click on the AF autofocus button and click "Capture to new page" button.

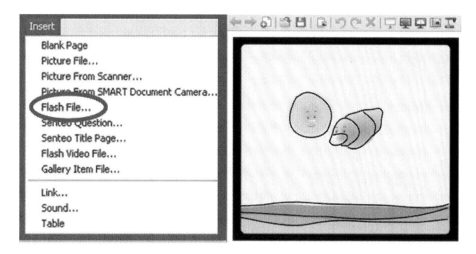

You can insert a **Flash File** like you would any picture. Notebook software reads SWF (Shockwave Flash) files. A fun Flash file to try is Calmbay1, a cheerful SWF file © Mandryka, 2003.

The accompanying music is from Marc Knopfler, from the soundtrack of the film Local Hero, © Phonogram 2003. You can download a compressed version of Calmbay1 at www.leconcombre.com/board/dl/us/Calmbay1us.html

When you insert a SWF into Notebook 10 software, it plays the first time you open the page. To play it again, quit Notebook and open it again.

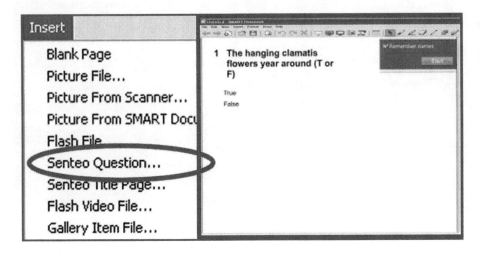

Insert Senteo Question lets you create questions for SMART's Senteo™ student response system even if you don't have the Senteo software drivers on your computer. You might want to create questions at home for delivery in your classroom.

It is easy to insert a **Senteo Question** into Notebook 10. The completed question is shown on the right.

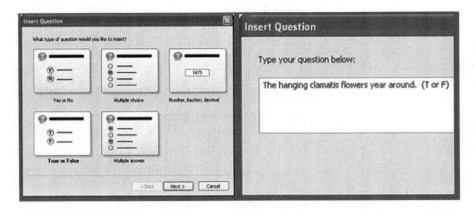

The Senteo Wizard will pop up. The first screen (shown at left) asks what type of question would you like to insert: Yes/No, Multiple choice, Number/fraction/decimal, True/False, Multiple answer. In this example, we clicked on True or False (it will be framed in red), and then clicked the Next button on the lower right corner.

The wizard prompts you to "type your question below:" We typed "The hanging clematis flowers year around. (T or F)."

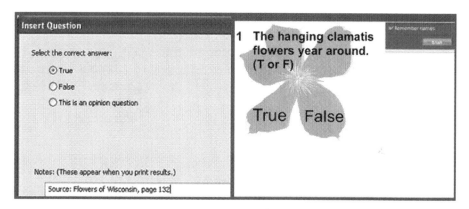

The wizard then prompts you to "Select the correct answer:" We clicked the radio button "False." You can use the Notes area if you wish. We wrote "Source: Flowers of Wisconsin, page 132" and clicked the "Finish" button. Normally, you would click the "Insert Another" button to add another question, and then click "Finish" when you are done entering questions.

On the right side of the image (above), you see the Senteo question AFTER we changed the font size, inserted the picture of a blue clematis that we scanned in with the SMART Document Camera, used the transparency layer tools to delete some shadows, selected the Properties tool to make the flower more translucent, clicked on the Object Menu to send the flower to the back, and moved the words True and False over the flower petals.

It is easy to use Notebook software for Senteo question creation. Notebook software is truly a highly graphical, flexible and simple courseware authoring tool.

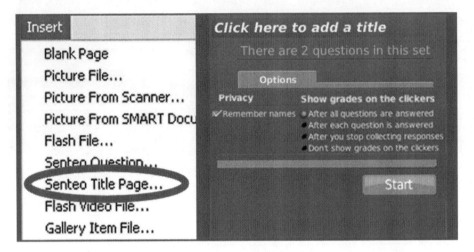

Once you have created Senteo questions, you need a Senteo Title Page to start the test. You choose the data gathering and feedback methods and "Start" the test. You can learn more about the Senteo response system and the SMART Document Camera in Simple SMART Skills, Volume 3.

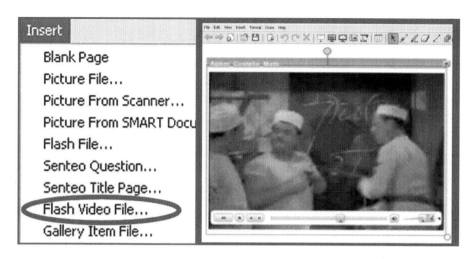

Notebook 10 supports FLV (Flash Video) and SWF (Shockwave Flash) video files. We have inserted a **Video File** from Teacher Tube in which Abbot and Costello take a zany approach to solving a math problem. Ask students to figure out why their math solution is wrong.

Downloading video from Teacher Tube and other websites is a challenge. Christopher Wright's "Edtechninja" blog gives great directions for converting Teacher Tube files into FLV files: http://edtechninja.com/smartboard/ask-the-tech-ninja-1-flash-video#comment-42

Notebook software inserts the movie player control panel into the video file when it is being played back via Notebook. At left are the familiar "VCR" pause, stop, rewind and forward commands, the slider to skip through the video, audio mute and volume controls. The right button is a still camera capture tool. The still image is captured on the same Notebook page and must be cut and copied onto a new page.

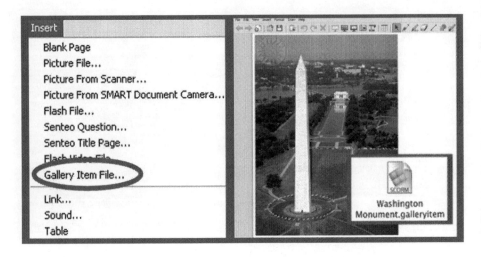

Most teachers will not use the Insert **Gallery Item File** command. But, suppose one of your friends (like us) converted images to Notebook Gallery item files. Dragging them from a storage device to a My Content folder in the Gallery tab, we would convert these items into Gallery item files. Then we would export and store them on a storage device (like a school's server) so you could Insert them as Gallery Item Files whenever you were using Notebook software.

Public.Resource.org downloaded 6,288 public domain images from the Smithsonian website, *smithsonianimages.si.edu* and made them available at http://bulk.resource.org/si.edu. We downloaded the zip tarball file, played around with the images and converted some into Gallery Item Files, such as Washington Monument.galleryitem.

Flickr is a great source for these images: http://www.flickr.com/photos/publicresourceorg/collections/72157600 214199993. A directory of the images is available from our publisher, Lulu: at http://stores.lulu.com/publicresource.

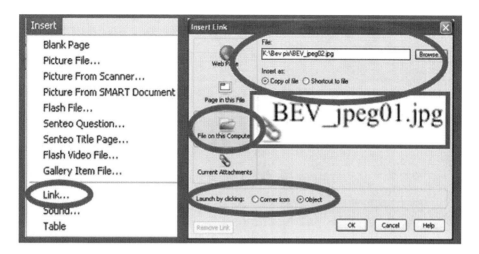

Normally, you create objects in Notebook software first, then link them individually via the Object Menu. However, if you are creating a table of contents, index or list page for your Notebook file, it is easier to use the Insert **Link** command.

In the above example, we created a Notebook file to supplement an art lecture, and are making a Notebook page listing paintings to display during the lecture. To do this, use images already scanned as JPEGs using the SMART Document Camera. Those images are saved to a hard drive.

Next, link to **File on this Computer**, and click on the **Choose File** button to browse to the file location. Insert each JPEG painting file into Notebook as a **Copy of File** (click the radio button), and **Launch** by clicking on the **Object** (click the radio button). When you click on **Insert Link**, a link is pasted into the upper left corner of the Noteboook page, with a paperclip showing that it is an attachment. By choosing Insert Copy of File, attach the file into this Notebook file.

Simply touch the file name to move it and click on the paperclip to launch it.

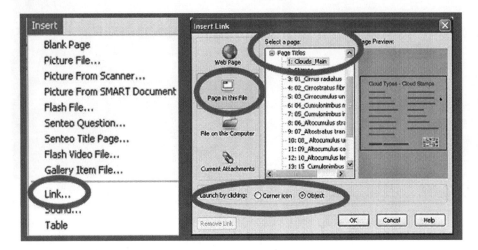

In the example above, you are linking to Page in this File, and have selected the page "Clouds Main" and Launch by clicking on the Corner Icon (click on radio button). .

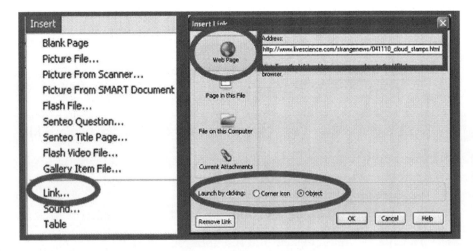

Above we linked to a web page, typing in a URL.

Notebook software for Windows supports MP3 files. There are many sources of free MP3 sound downloads on the internet. The sound used, "ohhh," came from www.a1freesoundeffects.com. You use the Insert menu and choose Sound, click on "Choose File" and browse to wherever on your computer you store sound files.

Here you see the upper left corner of a Notebook page, with the sound link "ohhh" pasted into it. Touch on the text to drag it into position, and touch on the speaker icon on the lower left corner play it.

If you want to make your own MP3s, a great free sound editing program is Audacity. Download it at www.audacity.sourceforge.net, and plug an inexpensive computer microphone into your Windows to start recording your own sounds.

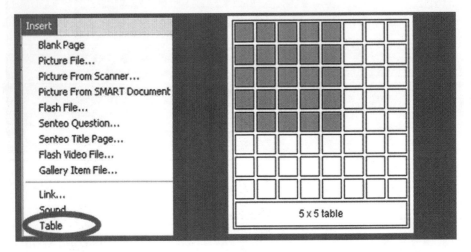

A new feature of Notebook 10 is the ability to insert a **Table**. See page 29-31 and 131-134 for complete details on creating tables.

Format Menu

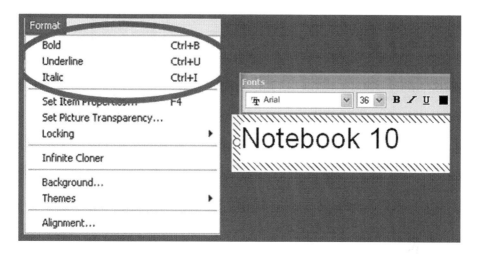

It is hard to understand the practical use of the first three commands on the format menu; unless you want to use Notebook software in conjunction with a voice activated assistive technology system for special needs students. Then you could select text with a switch-pointing system and then speak "Select, Text, Bold, Italic and Underline."

Most Notebook software users double tap on a word to select it, then highlight by sliding a finger over it. The Font menu appears and they touch on the B(old), I(talic) and U(nderline) buttons. But these format commands and the Control-B, -I and -U commands are there, if you ever need them.

Selected Item Properties... is also an unusual formatting command. Most users will click on a Notebook object and access Properties either by the Object Menu, the Properties Tab, or the Properties Tool. This is just one more way to access Properties.

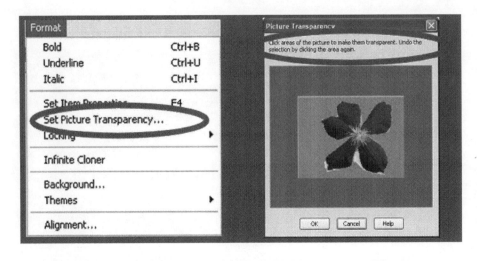

The Format pull down menu is the ONLY way to set **Picture Transparency**. In this example, we selected the blue clematis that we earlier scanned in with the SMART Document Camera. It's hard to see in black & white, but the area around the flower is violet, with some yellow shading. Click on the yellow areas around the object to make them violet. These violet areas are transparent. You notice at the bottom of the flower some yellow areas. These are shadow areas. You also need to click on to make them transparent.

Tip: click a few times to make some of the outside region transparent, then click on the **Set Transparency** button. Keep choosing Picture Transparency from the Format menu to work on the increasingly smaller areas to set transparent. There isn't Undo in this mode, so if you go too far, you will make some of the actual object transparent and will have to start all over again.

This is the finished blue clematis with shadows removed, set against a gradated green-to-light-green background. Picture transparency allows you to create much more lifelike manipulatives in your Notebook file.

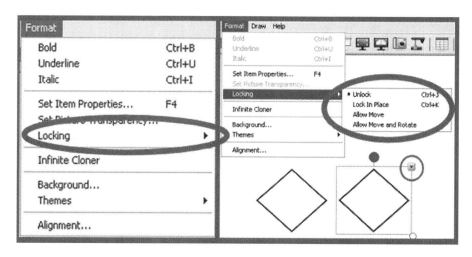

Locking objects keeps users from deleting them. You can lock in place, allow move, or allow move and rotate. More information on page 127.

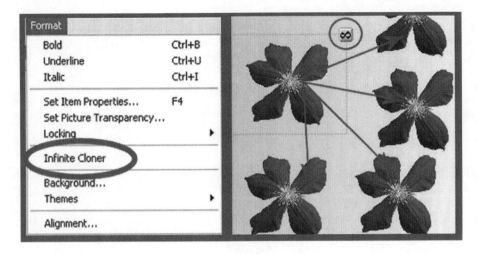

First introduced in Notebook 9, the **Infinite Cloner** is an easy way to make multiple image copies. Click on an object, choose Infinite Cloner from the Format menu and drag multiple copies from the original. Music teachers especially enjoy pulling quarter, half, three-quarter and full notes from the Gallery, creating an Infinite Cloner for each note, and positioning them on staves (in the Gallery).

Louise Weber, a Franklin, Wisconsin librarian, delighted us with a very visually creative Sudoku-like Notebook exercise using tiny animals from the Gallery, with Infinite Cloner "wells." Students dragged copies of the animals to fill in the "graphical" Suduko-like matrices. Other teachers have shared great infinite cloner examples of number, letter and word "wells" for cloze practice. To toggle off the cloner, touch the infinity symbol:

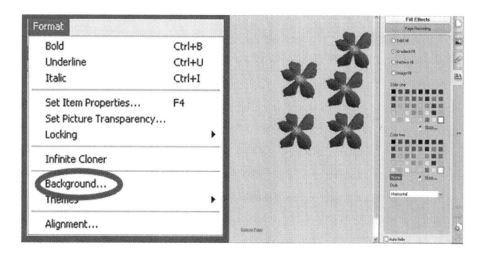

If you want to change **Background Color**, the easiest way is to touch and hold on the SMART Board for three seconds. This has the same results as doing a Right-Click. You can also change Background Color via the Format menu.

New to Notebook 10 software has multiple fill effects, including the standby Solid Fill, and the new **Gradient**, **Pattern** and **Image** fills. Click on the radio button to select your fill type. Here we have selected a yellow as Color One and light green as Color Two, with the color gradiating horizontally (left to right). Further details are covered in the Properties section on pages 160-173.

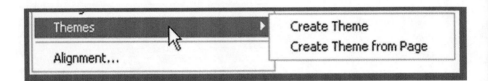

Themes are new to Notebook 10 and are a type of background that can be applied to a group of pages. Themes give your pages consistency, can help them look more polished, and can save you time.

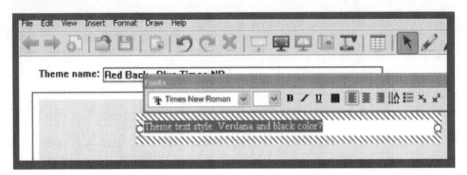

By choosing "Create Theme," you will get a white page with three areas to modify: Theme Name, Theme Text Style, and Background. Here, we are naming the theme "Red Back – Blue Times NR."

Double-tap on "Themes text style: Veranda and black color?" and the Text Properties Tool is displayed. Choose your font and color. Font size didn't seem to change, so ignore it. We made the text Times New Roman Blue.

Then right click on the white page area, to access the Page pull down menu, and "Set Background." We made the background a light red.

Finally, click the Save button on the bottom of the screen.

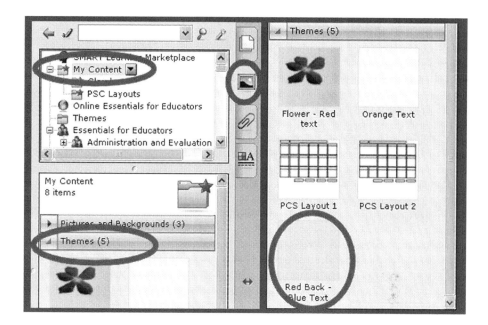

When you click on the Save button, the Theme is automatically saved into the Gallery's "My Content" folder. You can see the Themes you created in the Themes tab of the "My Content" view window.

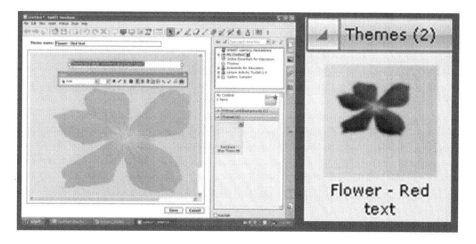

To "Create Theme from a Page," design your Notebook page, and use the same process as above.

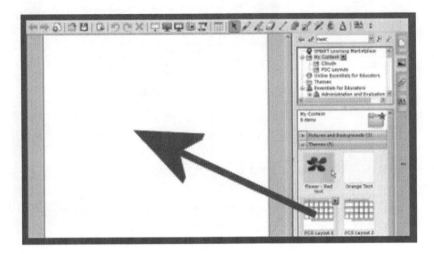

Here we are dragging a theme from the Gallery's My Content folder into a new Notebook file.

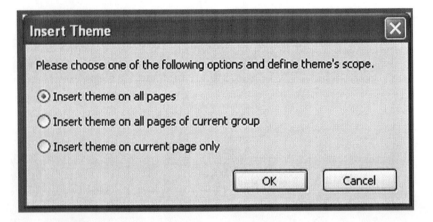

Once we drag the theme in, a dialog box asks how we want to apply the theme to the Notebook file. In this case, we will "Insert theme on all pages" and click the OK button.

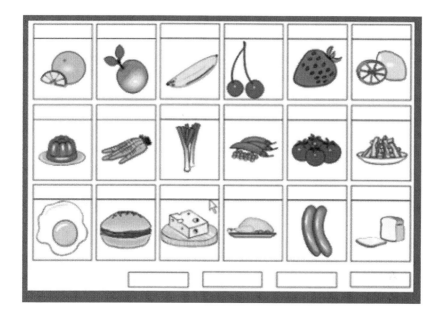

This project is a Notebook file for students with speech difficulties. They will click on multiple pages of the program to construct computer generated sentences. Sounds will be attached to the pictures, so users can come up to a specially designed SMART Board and touch the pictures to "speak."

The benefit of using Themes, is that themes creates a consistent background for us to use. We simply drag Gallery pictures onto the box. When we create a new Notebook page, the theme is automatically applied, and most of the new page is built for us.

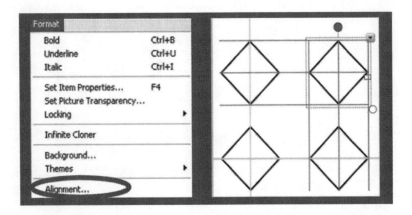

Alignment is also new to Notebook 10 software. Turn it on by selecting it from the Format menu. We created the diamond (in the lower left of the picture) and cloned three copies off it. Turning on all alignment options, we aligned the top left and lower right diamonds with the original. Finally, we positioned one in the upper right. The gray alignment grids show the horizontal and vertical centers of each diamond, and the red alignment grids are activated to help us drag the last (upper right) diamond into place. With Alignment, you can specify that Notebook objects will snap into place, helping you to create much more professional looking Notebook files.

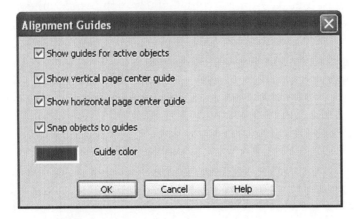

We usually leave alignment settings off, unless needed.

Draw Menu

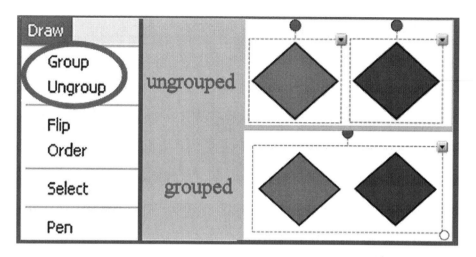

You can **Group** or **Ungroup** items by marqueeing them and then grouping them. When you use your finger on the SMART Board and you draw a box around several items to collectively select them, you are drawing a "marquee." Working at home using Notebook software on a computer WITHOUT a SMART Board interactive whiteboard attached, use your mouse to click the Select tool, then marquee (draw a frame around) the items you want to select.

Group (or ungroup) items with the Draw -> Group (Ungroup) menu command. You will probably find it more convenient to use the Object Menu to select commands for grouping items.

We use the grouping features a lot. In our "Mike's Moneybox" notebook file (page 2), we created a cash box using rectangles grouped together to simulate a cash register drawer, and finished it off with infinite clones of money and coins. These were gathered from the U.S. Treasury and Mint websites, using the Screen Capture tool.

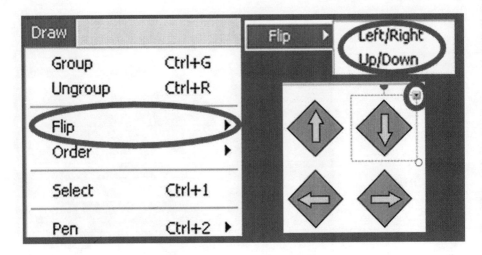

Flip an object up or down, left or right. In this example, using the Shapes Tool, we created a diamond, and filled it with green. We then created a yellow arrow, positioned it over the diamond, marqueed them and grouped the two objects together. From there, we cloned the object once, grabbed the second object by the handle and spun it 90 degrees. We marqueed both objects, cloned them, and used the alignment tool to perfectly position them. At this point we had two arrows pointing up, and two pointing left.

We selected the second "up-arrow diamond" and used the flip tool to flip it **Up/Down** to flip it 180 degrees into the down position. We then selected the second left diamond-arrow, and oddly enough, flipped it Up/Down.

You would think that you should flip it Left/Right, but since it was created with an up arrow, and then rotated 90 degrees using the green rotate handle, it has to be flipped down. Although confusing, that is the way it works.

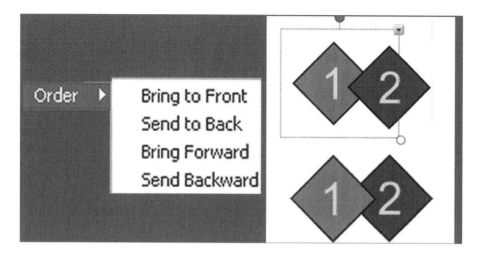

Order works very nicely in Notebook software. Every ungrouped object is in a different layer. Think of a Notebook page as having many different paper-thin transparencies sitting on top of each other. You move layers forward and backwards, one layer at a time, to achieve the desired appearance.

Using the Order command is simple. Select the red diamond with the number 1 on it (it is really two objects grouped together... the red diamond, and the yellow number 1), and you use the Draw->Order command **"Bring Forward"** to move it up one layer. If you **"Bring to Front,"** it becomes the top layer.

Draw has a **Select** command, but it is much more intuitive to simply make sure all the styluses are in the pen tray, then touch an object to select it. If you are working at the computer without a SMART Board interactive whiteboard attached, just use the mouse to click on the Select Tool, and then touch on the object.

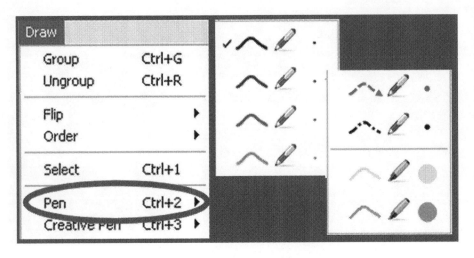

If you are an experienced Notebook 9 software user, the features shown on this page will be familiar. The **Pen** command from the Draw menu gives you the familiar Pen drop down menu. The only difference is that you can no longer customize from this drop down menu. You must use the Pen Tool and Properties Menu to do so.

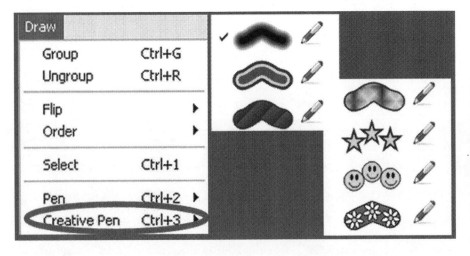

The Draw menu contains the familiar **Creative Pen** menu. You can also change Creative Pen widths, via the Creative Pen Tool custom Properties feature.

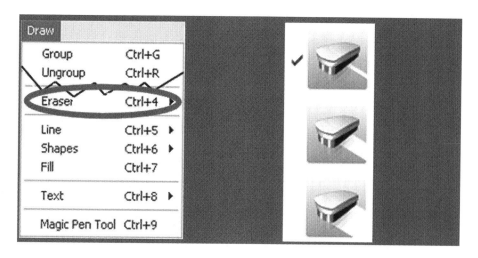

Again, via the Draw command, Notebook 9 users will have the familiar **Eraser** interface (page 34-35).

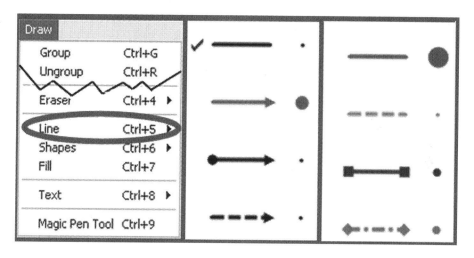

Our old friend, the Notebook 9 software **Line** interface. In Notebook 10 software, this is a little different. In Notebook 10 software, we customize lines via the Line Tool (page 36).

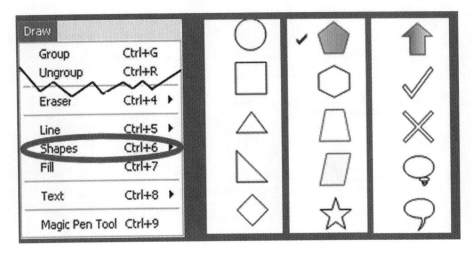

Ahha! Familiar territory... the **Shapes** menu (page 37-38), from Notebook 9. Customize with the Properties Tool.

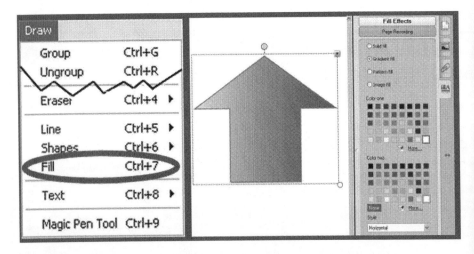

Above, you see something new... the **Fill** menu !!! A new Notebook 10 feature, use it to fill shapes. When you choose Fill, you get a Shapes Properties Menu. Click on your choices at the right, position the Paint Bucket, and touch to fill a shape. Make sure your computer is set to display 32-bit depth (millions of colors). You can set monitor display colors in Display Properties of the Windows System Preferences.

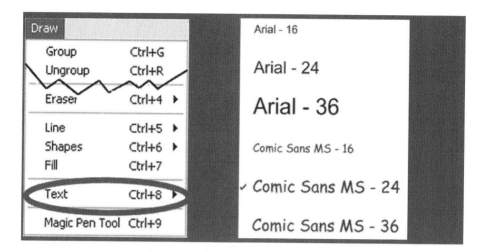

The **Text** menu is a quick way to access the top six font/size/styles that you have created in the Text Tool customization area. This feature will be very familiar to Notebook 9 software users.

The **Magic Pen** is covered on page 40-42.

The "Window" menu does not exist for Windows OS users, just for Macintosh. Windows and Windows OS computers handle Notebook files differently. On a Macintosh, you open one copy of Notebook software no matter how many Notebook files you want to work with. On a Windows PC, if you want to open a second Notebook file, you open a new copy of Notebook software from the Windows desktop.

On Windows, you juggle open files through the XP Task Bar, usually at the bottom of your computer screen, or via the File command on page 68.

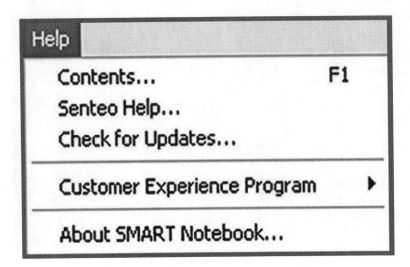

Help??? Maybe. The help in "**Contents...**" is NOT an easy read. There aren't a lot of pictures. You have to be connected to the internet to use it. Notebook software Help has a good index and search engine. This "help" is one of the many reasons we chose to write <u>Simple SMART Skills</u>.

Nevertheless, it IS a valuable reference tool regarding many of the more esoteric points of Notebook software. We referred to the online help several times in writing <u>Simple SMART Skills</u>. For example, who has in their head, what audio and video formats can be inserted into a Notebook file, where to find additional codecs and what file formats they will read??? But juicy tidbits like that ARE in Notebook software online help.

If you installed the Senteo student response system drivers, you will also have **Senteo Help**.

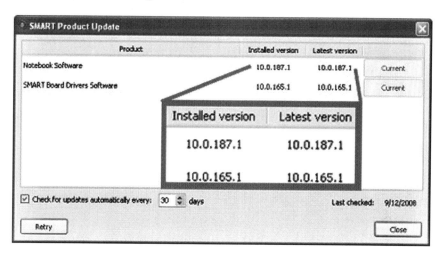

You can **Check for Updates** at the Help menu. However, your school's IT administrator may have safeguards in place to block you from updating your software. Here you see the version of Notebook Software and SMART Board Drivers software installed on our computer, and the latest version available. Any other SMART software installed on your system (e.g. Senteo, SMART Notebook Student Edition, etc.) would be listed here.

On the lower left corner of this update screen, you can set how often you want your computer to check for updates. Networked users may have this box unchecked.

Customer Experience Program tracks software crashes (rarely happens) and lets you email your ideas for future software features to SMART.

Use **About Notebook Software** to find what version of Notebook you are using. This book was written using Notebook Software for Windows, version 10.0.187.1, released on July 30, 2008.

Click on the **Technical Support** tab to see the version number of Notebook you are using and when it was created. Click this pop up window closed (red check box with on upper right corner of the pop up window), to get back to Notebook software.

If you ever have to call SMART Technical Support (888-42-SMART), it is helpful to tell the support technician what version of Notebook software and what computer operating system you are using.

If learning about Notebook software menus is like eating a great meal, learning about the secret right-click at the end of the Tools is like having a great dessert. We are always delighted by the new features of each new release of Notebook software, but are sometimes overwhelmed by the increasing complexity of the application. So, when you right-click on the tool bar, you can customize the Notebook Toolbar.

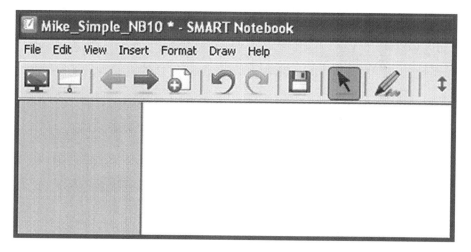

With **Customize Toolbar**, you can create simpler toolbars, with less clutter, to provide a simpler toolset that gives users just what they need. Think of a second grade classroom, a special education situation, or even a new Notebook user training session. You might want a simple set of tools to get to the core of Notebook software.

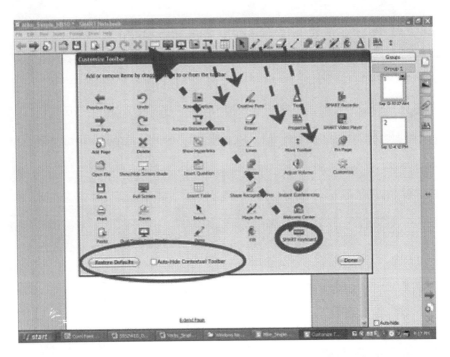

When you select Customize Tools, simply drag the tools you do not need off the Tool Menu. If you don't like the order of the tools, just drag them to a better location.

Auto-hide Contextual Toolbar is a new feature on the lower left corner of this screen. Just click the checkbox to turn this feature on.

The Macintosh Customize Toolbar is a little nicer, because there you can create Notebook files with different toolbars. On Windows, you are actually changing the application tools. However, it is nice to create a simpler Notebook application, and graduate on to bigger toolsets when you (or your students) are ready.

5

Object Menus

This simple doodle and everything else you write, drag or paste onto your SMART Board interactive whiteboard is an object. When you touch an object, you will see the Object Menu. It is accessible via the triangle at the selected object's upper right corner. Touch and pull down to reveal the Object Menu. Other than the styli ("pens") and eraser, the Object Menu is the most seamless and intuitive part of the Notebook interface. It is usually the fastest way to interact with Notebook objects.

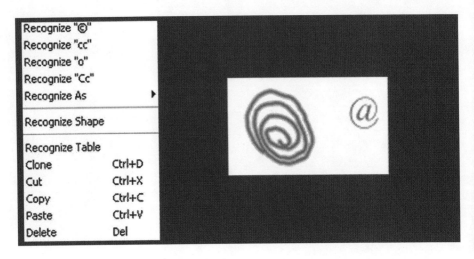

When you write with a pen, the first Object Menu command is **Recognize** handwriting. The four closest guesses are usually listed. Here, we touched "Recognize @" and converted the doodle to an ampersand. The Windows version recognizes both printed and cursive text.

Recognize As lets you recognize a word in a foreign language. Touch Recognize As and then select a language (we chose French), even though we were using Notebook software in English. The text was deliciously converted to "bon appétit." This is a new feature of Windows Notebook 10 software.

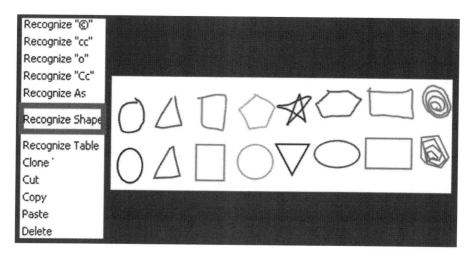

New to Notebook 10 software is the ability to **Recognize Shape**s. On the top line of the above screen shot, we have drawn shapes. By touching or clicking on Recognize Shape, these are converted to the shape graphics you see on the lower line. Notebook recognizes ovals, circles, triangles, rectangles, and squares.

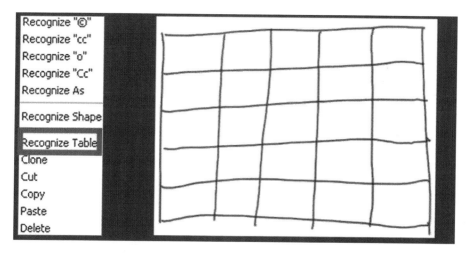

Notebook 10 software has a Recognize Table feature, to interpret freehand table sketching. It is not perfect. We rather just build a table from scratch or copy and paste one in from Microsoft Excel™.

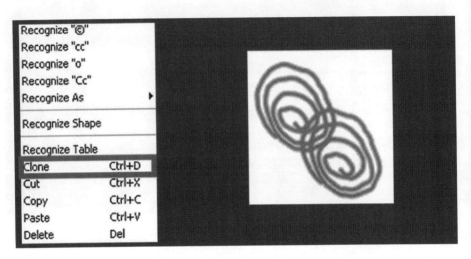

The **Clone** command is simply a one-step version of **Copy** and **Paste**. These familiar Windows commands, as well as **Cut** and **Delete** are self-explanatory. Anything you can copy from another program into the Windows Clipboard, you can paste into Notebook.

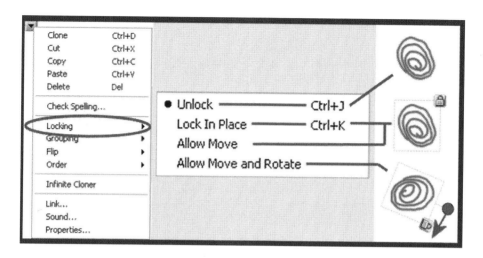

Locking allows you "some" protection from others modifying your work. Notebook's open-source approach lets you look at other Notebook files and unlock locked items to modify them as you desire.

The Flash animations used in many Notebook files cannot be modified, unless they are files created with Lesson Activity Toolkit content. LAT files are extensively covered in our book,"Simple SMART Skills, Vol. 1, For Teacher Productivity and Student Engagement."

When you click on an object and lock it, a padlock appears where the Object Menu triangle previously existed. You can **Lock in Place** to keep an object stationary, **Allow Move** to allow students to manipulate but not delete, and **Allow Move and Rotate**, using the last command causes the green rotate handle to appear.

Remember, you can Select All Locked Notes from Edit command (page 72) to see where all locked objects are on any Notebook page.

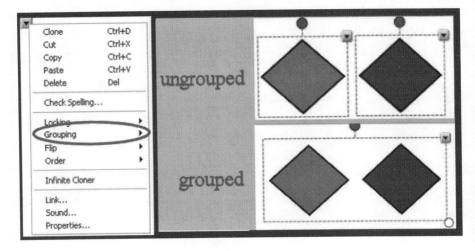

Grouping is covered on page 111. Rather than using the Grouping command, we find it easier to marquee objects, then select Grouping from the Object Menu, because it is easily accessible.

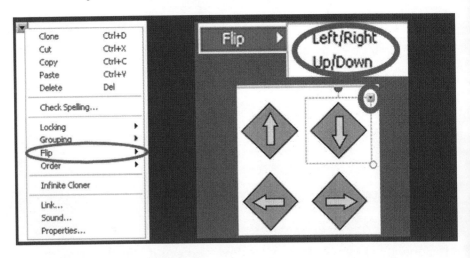

Flip is covered on page 112.

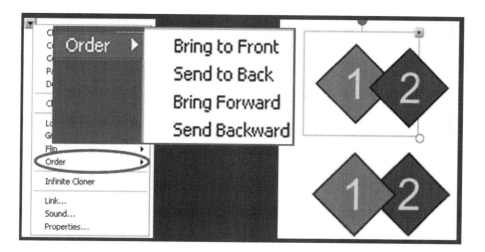

Order is covered on page 113.

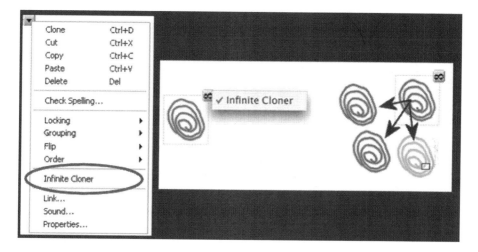

Infinite Cloner is covered on page 104.

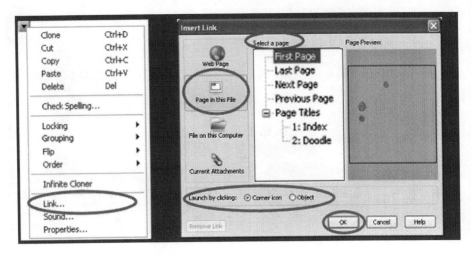

Link is covered on pages 97-98.

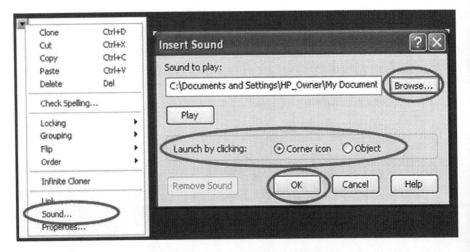

Sound is covered on page 99-100. You cannot command an object to link and play a sound simultaneously. You can create an object that links when you click on the object, and play a sound when you click on the corner icon.

Object Menus

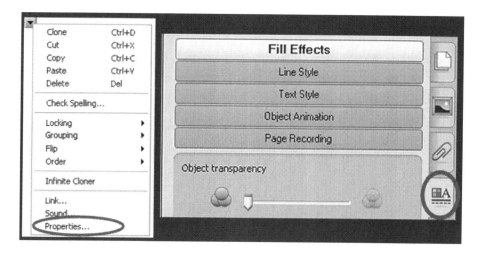

Properties are extensively covered in the Properties Tab section on pages 160-173.

Tables

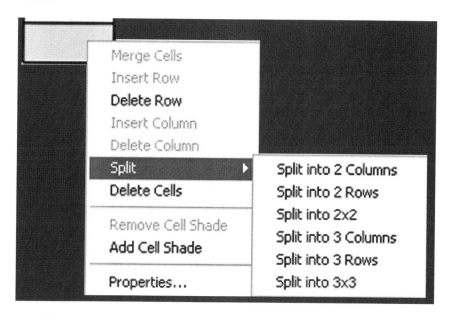

When you select a table cell and then Control click on it (touch the Virtual Right Mouse button on the pen tray and then touch a table cell) you access the Object Menu for the Table Cell.

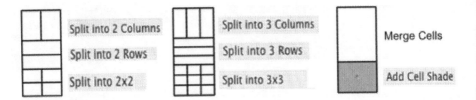

On a Windows using Notebook 10 software, you can create a 8x8 matrix table. However, you can manipulate each cell in various ways, as shown above.

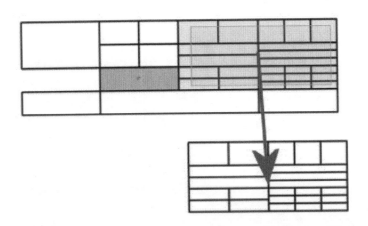

In this above example, we have created a 4x4 table and manipulated each cell to illustrate different looks you can create with cells. You can also highlight a matrix section and pull off a copy. We used the Select Tool, and created a marquee in the area bounded by the thin green line, which highlighted the active cells (3x2 matrix) in gray, which we then touched and dragged.

The largest table you can create with Notebook 10 software on a Windows is 8x8. To create a larger table, we used a trick. We create several tables, highlight them, then use keyboard arrow keys to very closely position them. They will appear to be one large table, (example on page 161). But, you will know the tables are separate if you try to highlight cells of different tables, because you cannot highlight cells of both tables at the same time.

Using several Notebook tools together can make for spectacular use of tables. Here we used the Animal Sudoku idea of our librarian friend, Louise Weber. We created a 3x3 table, split each cell into 3x3 (another technique for creating large tables), used Properties to shade each 3x3 and made the shading transparent. We dragged nine birds from the Gallery, resized the birds, and positioned our flying friends with Alignment, and made each an infinite clone.

We then took the Sudoku game from the Gallery's Lesson Activity Toolkit, hitting the solve button, taking a Screen Capture, resizing it and pulling it onto this page (cover it with a white filled shape to hide and reveal the solution). This Notebook took about an hour to create, but by saving along the way, we can easily create additional Animal Sudoku pages.

6

Notebook Tabs

Notebook 10's Notebook Tabs are the **Page Sorter**, **Gallery**, **Attachments** and **Properties**.

The four tabs appear above. They will be located on the far right or left side of the screen. Earlier versions of Notebook software had tabs with text labels "Page Sorter," "Gallery," with the "Attachments" tab added in Notebook 8. The "Properties" tab is new to Notebook 10. Expect to see additional tabs as SMART Technologies adds new functionality to Notebook software.

Page Sorter Tab

When you add a new page to Notebook software, the page is automatically time and date stamped.

To title the page, first touch the **Page Sorter** tab, then touch the Page, and lastly touch the page title (which would be Dec 23-6:57 PM). When you touch the page title, the text is highlighted. Type in the new title "Biblio w/links" to name this page, using your computer keyboard or the virtual keyboard.

The active page will be highlighted with a blue rectangle.

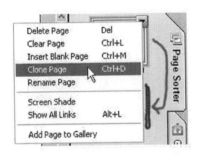 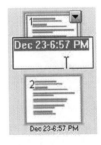 

Clone Page is another way to create a new page. Use the Object Menu to clone a page. (Here we are seeing an example from Notebook 9, but the concept is still the same.)

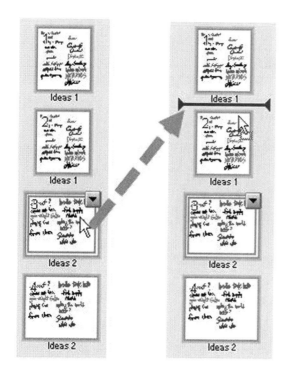

Using the Page Sorter tab, you can easily reposition page thumbnails, dragging them to reorder. The pages, shown above, have different widths because the "Ideas 1" page is actually more than one full screen in height. When we were brainstorming ideas in Notebook, we clicked on the "Extend Page" at the bottom of the "Ideas 1" page. In the Page Sorter, each page thumbnail is always the same height. The skinnier the page, the longer it is.

Sometimes you will delete information on a page, and it will still appear skinny in the Page Sorter. Just touch a different page thumbnail, and the page you were working on will resize.

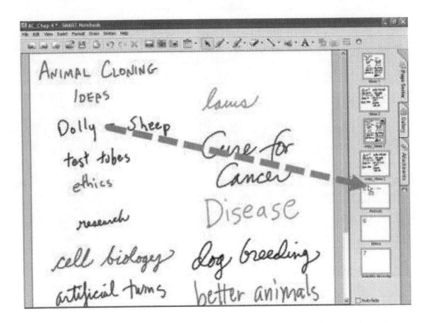

Another use for the Page Sorter is to drag information from a page onto a thumbnail. One of our favorite Notebook whole class activities is a process writing activity where every student comes to the board and writes an idea for a theme. Then we create pages to classify their ideas and have students drag their ideas into the appropriate page. We finish the exercise by clicking on each classification page, and have students move the ideas around to reorder them. During the activity, we ask students to write additional brainstorming ideas for their theme as seatwork, and in the end, print (or PDF and email) the brainstorming activity as a story skeleton for students to use for writing their theme.

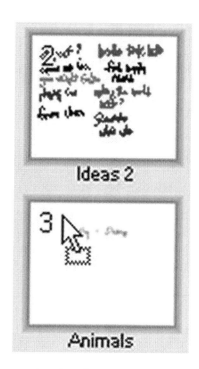

On the above "Animals" page, you see a pointer and a miniature representation of the text as we drag it to the thumbnail. This gives visual feedback that the Notebook object is being moved.

Why you should have named pages

In the example below, we have created a new Notebook file with a mix of additional and subtraction problems. These pages we called "program_1…"

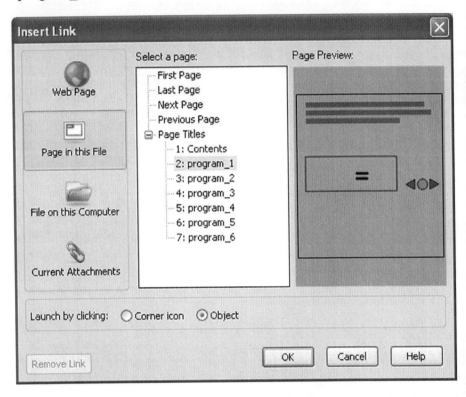

One reason to name pages is to make linking easier. If all the pages are merely time and date stamped, it is hard to figure out which page to link to. In the page sorter, when you replace a thumbnail page's time and date stamp with a title, the "page title" shows up when linking pages.

Groups

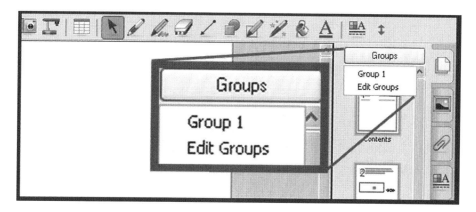

Groups is a new Notebook 10 feature. Click on the Group box at the top of the Page Sorter area to access the **Edit Groups** command.

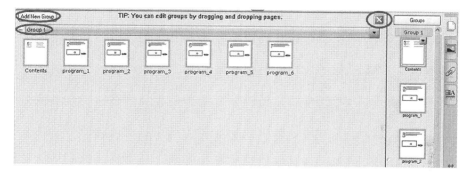

When you click Edit Groups you see the above window in Notebook. By default, there is one group in Notebook, called Group1. To add another group, click the **Add Group** button in the upper left corner. At the top center, you have directions to "Edit your groups by using drag and drop." The circled red close box on the upper right exits you back to normal Notebook mode.

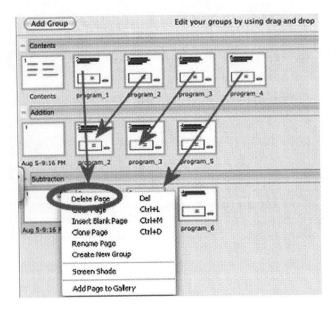

Above, we have created two new groups - "Addition" and "Subtraction." We dragged each page to the correct group (program 2, 3, and 5 have addition problems) (program 1, 4, and 6 have subtraction problems).

When a new group is created, a blank page is also created. After forming your groups, use the thumbnail page's Object Menu to delete these unneeded pages. You can also quickly create Screen Shades for each page from this Object Menu.

If you create large Notebook files, groups can help you organize your Notebook file.

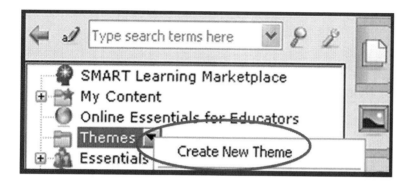

Themes are new to Notebook 10. A theme is a background/text style combination applied to a page, group or all Notebook pages. Think of a theme as a background template.

Access themes through the Gallery tab. Click on the Themes folder, then use the Themes folder Object Menu to "Create New Theme."

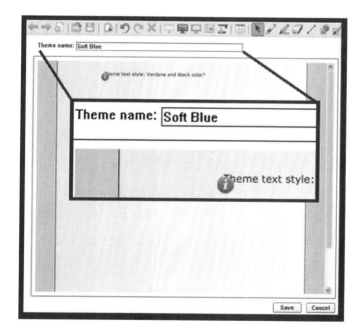

Name the theme and select a Theme text style. Click the "Save" button on the bottom right corner of the Theme creation window.

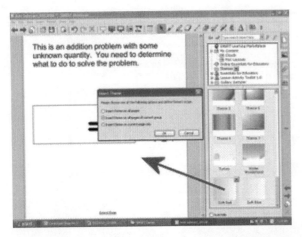

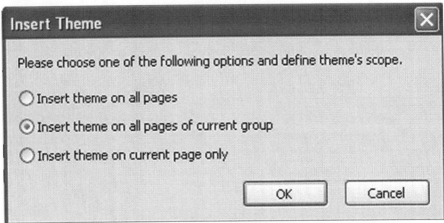

Your new theme appears in the Gallery's "My Content" Themes folder. To use it on a page or group of pages, pull the theme onto the page. The "Insert Theme" dialog box appears. In the example above, we clicked the radio button "Insert theme on all pages of the current group." This gave all the addition pages a red background. We dragged in a blue theme for the subtraction pages, in the same manner. This gives students a visual cue to help them solve the word problems you created, by associating the page color with an arithmetic function.

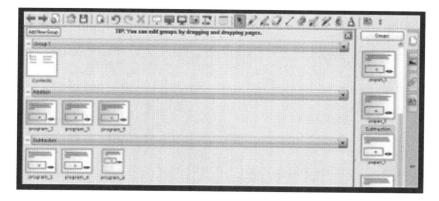

In the above illustration of the page sorter, you see the themes applied to each group.

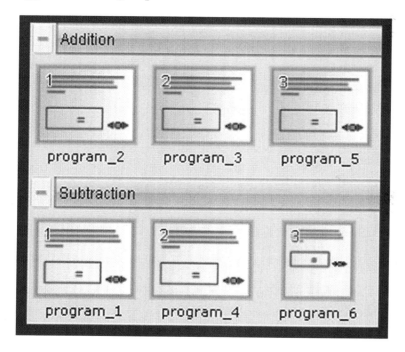

Here is a close up view of the page groups, with a red background for addition and blue for subtraction problems.

Gallery Tab

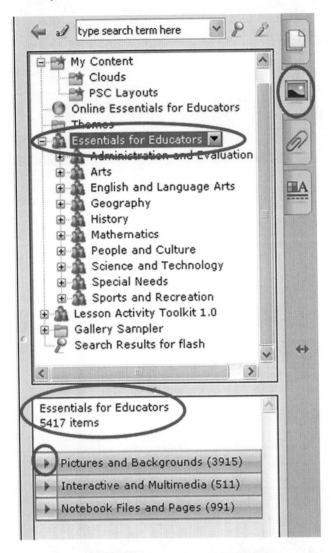

The Gallery contains a wealth of graphic images. The Gallery is a searchable database of graphics and other objects that you can use with all SMART Notebook files. Essentials for Educators contains over 600 MB that is 5,400 pieces - clip art, including pictures, backgrounds, multimedia, Flash animation, graphics with attached sounds, SMART Notebook files and more.

You can customize the Gallery via the "My Content" folder. Move frequently used Gallery content as well as imported media files to your "My Content" folder. You can also export "My Content" folders to share with others. Schools can set up shared "Team Content" folders on servers for teacher and student use.

When you click on a particular Gallery folder, you view the content in the lower "Search Results" window.

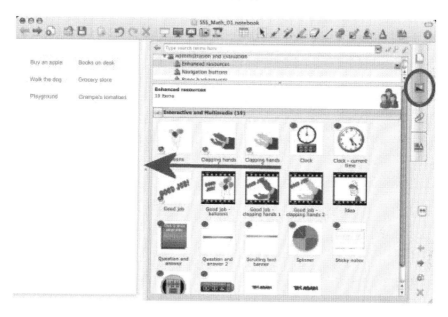

Gallery tab windows can be resized. In the above example, we dragged the upper right search window to make it very short, and the entire Gallery window very wide. This lets us see as many Gallery items as possible. Here we are looking at interactive and multimedia Gallery items (primarily Flash animations) in the Administration and Evaluation folder of the Essentials for Educators Gallery.

Each subject area in the Essentials for Educators Gallery folder has subcategories. To get to a subcategory, click on the "plus mark" in front of the appropriate folder. It works very much like navigating in folders with Windows OS.

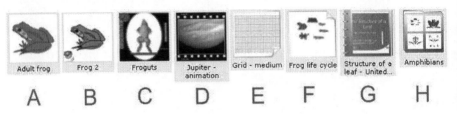

These are the different types of objects in SMART Notebook Gallery:

A – **Object**. Could be text, SMART notebook object (e.g. shape) or a graphic image (JPG or BMP)

B – **Graphic image with audio file attached** (Click on the speaker to play the sound.)

C – **Flash animation** (usually interactive)

D – **Computer movie**

E – **Background** (You can draw over it. When you erase, the background remains.

F – **Notebook page** (You can draw over it. When you erase, the page remains)

G – **Notebook file** (multi-page lesson)

H – **Folder** containing Gallery objects

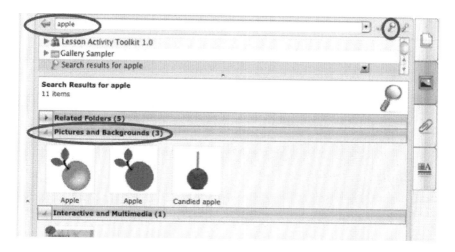

You can search the Gallery by typing in a keyword, then clicking on the Magnify Glass (looks like a Windows search icon) or by pressing the Return key on your computer keyboard. In the "apple" example, above, three pictures and background have come up, along with one interactive and multimedia element. We have clicked on the triangle in front of Pictures and Backgrounds to see the three Gallery items.

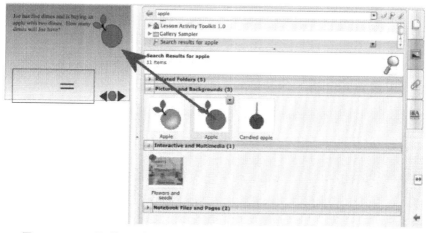

To move a Gallery item to a Notebook page, simply drag it to the page.

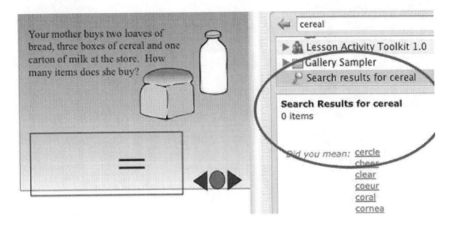

We have inserted bread and milk into the above Notebook page, but found no search results for "cereal."

It is easy to add your own content to the Gallery "My Content" folder. You can drag JPGs from websites to the XP Task Bar. Keep your finger in contact with the SMART Board interactive whiteboard, and drag it into the "My Content" folder, or a subfolder you previously created via the "My Content" Object Menu.

"My Content" folders also allow you to take objects, including JPG and BMP images, from other sources and bring them into the Gallery. On the screen shown on the previous page, using a web browser, we have dragged images of coins from http://www.wpclipart.com, a public domain image collection, into the Gallery. Before bringing objects into your "My Content" folder, make sure you do the following: open a SMART Notebook file on your computer, select the Gallery tab, and open the subfolder where you want to store the object.

To do this on the SMART Board, using the Safari browser, simply drag the penny to the Windows task bar and then into the Gallery folder Search Results window.

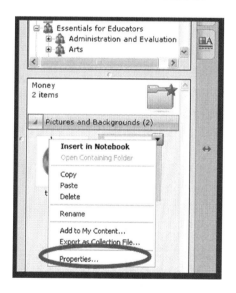

Once you have moved the images to the Money folder, go to the Gallery Search Results window. Right click on the penny and rename it if you wish. Do this by editing the name below the object. (You can also do this by dragging to Rename or by clicking on the Object Menu and drag to Properties.)

Below, we are selecting Properties for the dime.

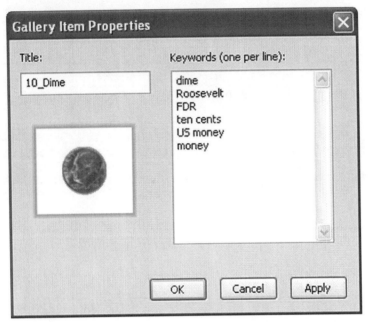

In the Properties box, you can type in search terms. Press return after each search term you enter. Click **Apply** to save your work. This is how you can set up search keywords for clipart.

Some of our favorite Gallery items include:

Rolling dice. Although you can use this for a probability lesson, you can also use the dice to randomly call on students. One die can signify the row and the other the column in your seating chart. Students often enjoy being called on randomly, and report that it is "more fair" than having the teacher select students to come to the SMART Board.

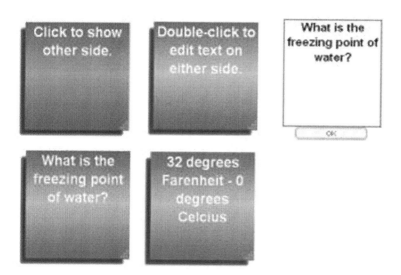

Question and answer. Make a Jeopardy™-style game or other drill and practice with this Flash object. Here you see the steps for using this "flipping" question/answer tile.

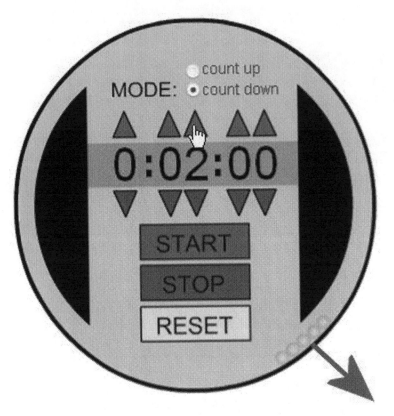

Timer. Use the timer for classroom work and tests. Click on the green (up) triangles to set the clock upwards, or red (down) triangles to set the clock downwards. Click the green start button to start the timer, STOP to pause it. (The five translucent dots on each of the SMART Gallery Flash objects allow you to resize the image.) If you have speakers attached to your computer, the timer will beep when time's up.

Clock face. Great for primary time-telling work. Pick up a pen and write down the correct time on the SMART Board. Point to any hand and drag it around the clock face.

Fraction maker. The Fraction Maker converts your handwriting to a fraction. Drag it from the Gallery onto the SMART Board, pick up a pen and write the numerator and denominator. Your handwriting will be converted to text. Click on the big arrow, and a fraction will be created. The fraction is now an object which you can drag around the screen.

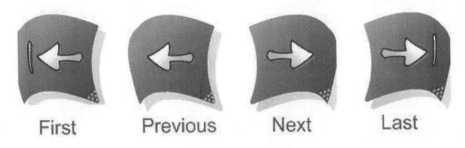

First   Previous   Next   Last

Flash navigation buttons. Add these Gallery Flash navigation buttons to your SMART Notebook file to move from page to page without creating links.

Flip a coin. A heads or tails decision making tool, to add fun and interest to your lectures.

A great way to learn new ways to use a SMART Board interactive whiteboard is to do a Gallery search on "Flash," and play with the several hundred Flash items in the Gallery.

Research shows that teachers' ability to easily access the thousands of Gallery items saves prep time and assists in helping the teacher prepare quality presentations.

The Lesson Activity Toolkit (LAT) is an optional download for the Gallery. The LAT is extensively covered in <u>Simple SMART Skills: Vol. 1</u>.

Attachments Tab

The **Attachments tab** appears as a paperclip (top right). The **Insert** button is at the bottom, with three insert options.

Notebook's Attachments Tab allows you to attach any computer file to your Notebook presentation. You can create (or modify) a Notebook file for your class period lecture, and attach word processing documents, PDF worksheet files, scanned JPG images, URL web links, and Windows Media Video (WMV) movies... any data files which you have application software on your computer to display. The Attachments Tab makes your Notebook file quite an organizational tool.

We like to compare the Attachment Tab to the file cabinets our best teachers had – full of well used and honed overhead transparencies that they used year after year. These teachers would pull out their overheads and notes out for the day's lecture, with everything organized in one place.

Notebook files with attachments let you do the same thing for high tech teaching. Create your presentation in Notebook software, adding attachments by clicking on the Insert button at the bottom of the Attachments window.

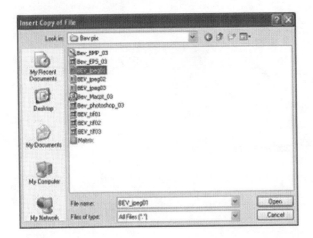

When you attach a file using the paperclip icon, you can choose to insert a copy of the file, or create an alias that points to a file on a storage device. We believe it is almost always better to insert a copy of the file into your Notebook page. The only exception is if you are inserting a very large file (like a 400MB digital movie).

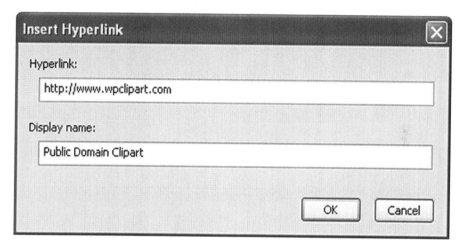

Before you attach a hyperlink, it is best to open up a web browser (Safari, Firefox, Internet Explorer, Google Chrome, etc.) and test your URL before attaching it. Type the URL into the browser. When you are sure it has gone to the correct page, highlight and copy it. Paste it into the Notebook hyperlink box, above, as we did on the previous page. If you want, you can type in a different display name to make it easier to find the link the next time.

Properties Tab

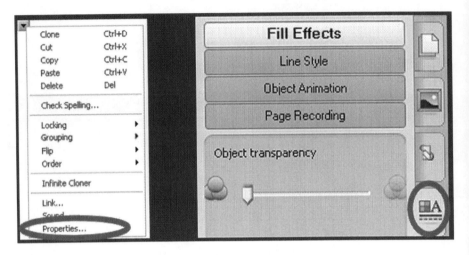

When you set object **Properties**, you are determining how they will appear in Notebook software. There are three ways to define object properties in Notebook 10 software: by selecting the object and pulling down on the Object Menu to Properties; by selecting the object and touching on the Properties Tool at the upper right corner of the Tool Menus; or by selecting the Object and clicking on the Properties tab.

	A	B	C	D	E	F	G	H	I
Background		■						■	
Pen	■		■	■	■	■		■	
Magic Pen		■	■	■		■		■	
Creative Pen		■	■	■		■		■	
Eraser		■	■	■	■	■	■	■	
Line		■	■		■	■	■	■	
Shape	■	■	■	■	■	■		■	
Shape Recog.			■	■	■		■	■	
Fill	■	■		■	■	■	■	■	
Text	■		■	■	■	■		■	
Insert Picture	■							■	

A – Fill Effects – Object Transparency

B – Fill Effects – Fill Style

C – Line Style – Thickness

D – Line Style – Color

E – Line Style – Style

F – Line Style – Start/End

G – Text Style

H – Object Animation

I – Page Recording

The table above shows the different properties for different Notebook objects. We will explore each of these properties in more detail on the following pages.

Fill Effects

On page 90, we scanned in a blue clematis with a SMART Document Camera, and used it in a Senteo question we created on page 93. The Properties Fill Effects – Transparency Layer was used to make the flower transparent, allowing the text could be readable over it.

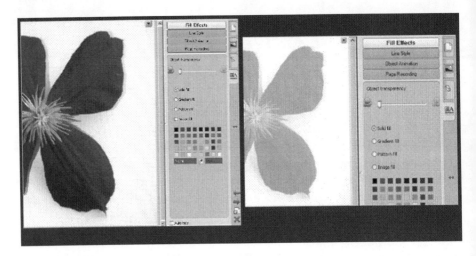

To use fill effects, touch the object to select it, click on the Properties tab, choose the Fill Effects tab, and select the desired Object Transparency level. The image immediately changes its' appearance, helping you determine exactly what level of transparency you desire. Because the flower is a Notebook object, you can make changes to the object's properties at any time.

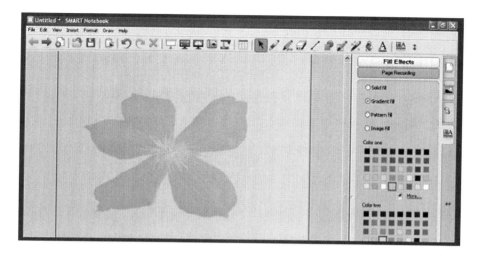

Backgrounds and the Fill Tool have Fill Style as a Fill Effect option. If you are sharing Notebook files with Notebook 9 software users, use only Solid Fill. If you use any other fill option (e.g. gradient fill), when a Notebook 9 user opens your Notebook 10 file, the fill color will not show.

If you are creating your Notebook file to run on Notebook 10 software only, you can use gradient, pattern or image fills. In this example, Color 1 is dark green and Color 2 is yellow, and we used Horizontal style, so the color gradient changes from left to right. We also used Picture Transparency on the flower (pages 102-103) to make invisible the white background surrounding the flower.

Line Style and Fill Effects

Most Notebook objects allow you to set a variety of Line Style effects (see table on page 161).

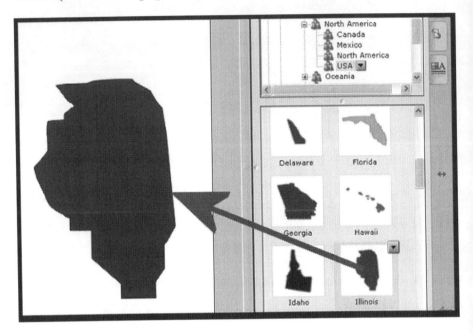

On page 40, we illustrated a gradient shade, which we used to shade the state of Illinois. You can pull the image out of the Gallery (Essentials For Educators -> Geography -> Maps -> North America -> USA -> Pictures and Backgrounds). Then touch Illinois to select it, and resize it as desired.

Touch the Properties tab, then touch the Line Style button, and select the line thickness and color you want for the Illinois outline.

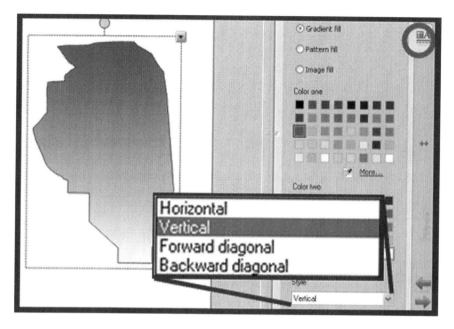

To set fill effects on the image, touch the Fill Effects button. Choose Gradient Fill (select the radio button in front of Gradient Fill), choose Color One and Color Two and finish up by determining your gradient style (the direction you want the gradient from Color One to Color Two).

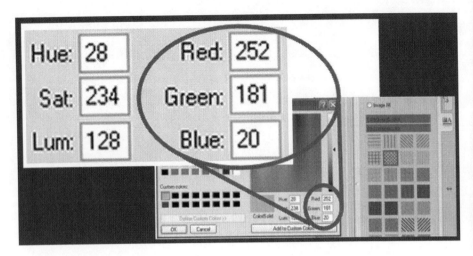

Want to make Wisconsin Green and Gold? Drag the image of
Wisconsin from the Gallery, select it, click on the Properties Tab, and
choose Pattern Fill. Touch on Foreground Colour and pick your color.
The RGB colors for the Green Bay Packers colors are (Green R:33
G:61 B:48 and Gold R:252, G:181, B:20.)

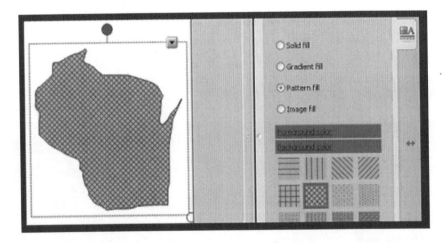

Above, we chose a yellow background color and added an X-
hatched pattern.

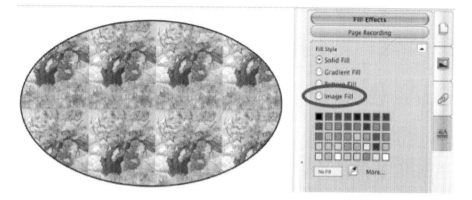

Image fill lets you insert a picture into a Shape.

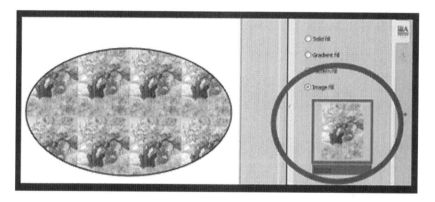

In Properties, click on the Image Fill radio box, then touch the Browse button. An Open dialog box lets you select an image which you can insert into a shape. This takes a bit of experimentation, because your results will vary depending upon the image and shape sizes. A large image is cropped into the object, whereas a small image repeats itself, as shown in the "cameo" example, above.

You can also insert an image and click on the "Eyedropper" to choose colors that exactly match your art. Above, we selected the eyedropper and clicked on a tree trunk to create Colour One, and chose white for Colour Two, to create this gradient background.

You can also click on "More" under Properties Colour One. Chose the Picture palette, select an image, and match any color you want.

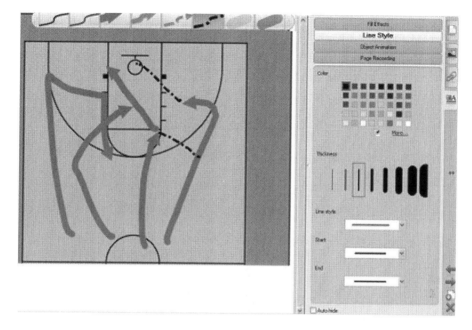

Lines and pens have Line Thickness, Style, Start and End points as part of Line Style. In the example above, we have pulled a half basketball court out of the Sports and Recreation file in the Essentials for Educators (Gallery). The dotted lines show where two players pass the ball. If you like the new pen design, click the **Save Tool Properties** button and that pen changes in the Pens menu.

If you are a physical education teacher or coach, using Notebook software for X and O play diagramming is another of the many versatile uses of this program. We just hope that your plays are better designed than ours.

This same technique can be used by a social studies teacher showing the progress of French exploration in Canada, an earth science teacher discussing ocean current flow, a physics teacher lecturing on motion studies, or a kindergarten teacher asking a student to diagram how to get to the library.

Multiple width Creative Pens is a new Properties feature in Notebook 10 software.

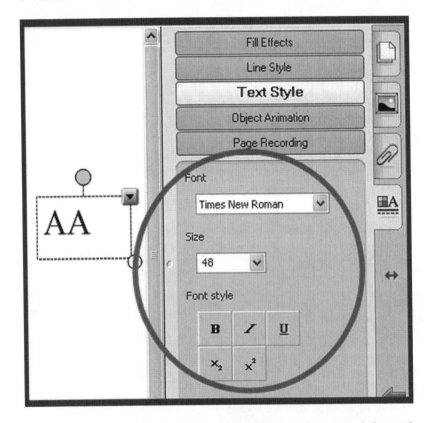

Text, created either with the Text tool, or converted through handwriting recognition, can be modified with Text Style in the Properties pull down menu. Options include changing the font, size and style.

Object Animation

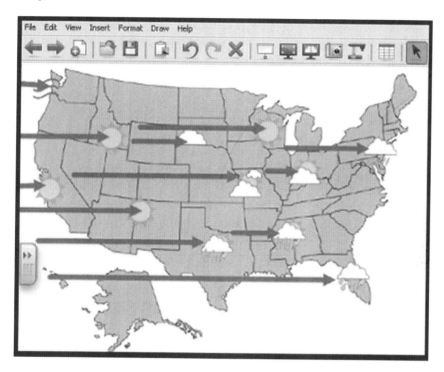

Let your imagination go in Notebook 10. After watching a TV weather forecaster click on maps and "fly in" temperatures, we decided to try it in Notebook software! The Gallery's Essentials for Educators gave us all the clip art needed, with a U.S. map from the Geography folder and weather symbols from the Science and Technology / Earth Science folder. After dragging in the gallery objects, we touched them, one at a time, and then selected **Object Animation**.

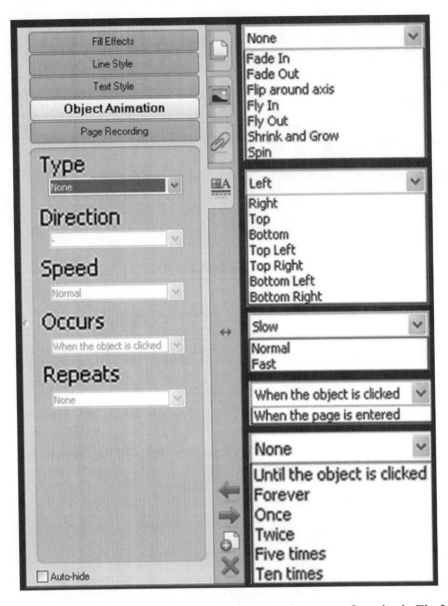

Although there are other types of animations, our favorite is Fly In (Type), Left (Direction), Normal (Speed), When the page is entered (Occurs), None (Repeats). Just play until you master this.

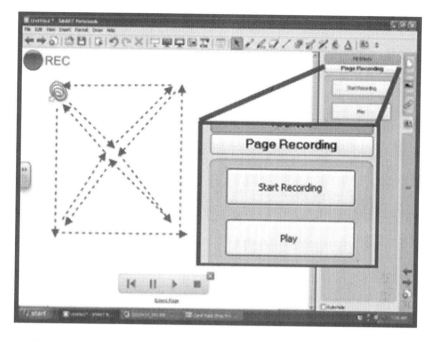

Page Recording, another new Notebook 10 software feature, lets you record anything on a Notebook page. If you wanted to work and "replay" math problems (or any other whiteboarding activity) for study, and imbed your recording into Notebook, you can now do this.

Click on Properties, the Page Recording tab, and the red Recording "light" is displayed in the upper left corner of your active Notebook page. The **Replay Control Bar** is also displayed. Move any Notebook objects around and they are recorded. Click the square Stop button in the Replay Control Bar, or the Play button in the Page Recording tab to stop recording. Click Play (right pointing triangle) to play back. Sound is not recorded in this initial release of Notebook 10 software… but it sure would be a nice feature. (You can record sound in SMART Recorder software, see page 204-205.)

7

Advanced Tools

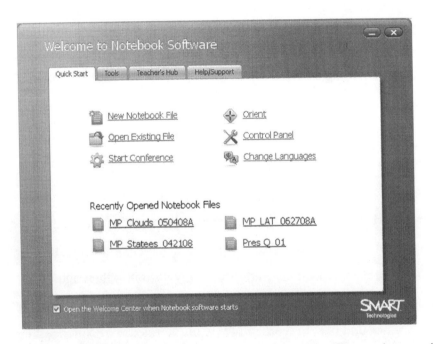

The Welcome Center is the gateway for controlling and accessing many Notebook Tools. Welcome Center basics were covered in Chapter 2. We will now explore the more advanced features of the Welcome Center, starting with the Control Panel.

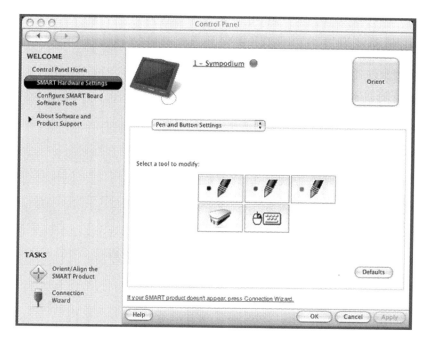

When you touch the Control Panel link, this screen shows you which SMART products you have connected to your computer. In this example, we have a Sympodium™ interactive monitor attached to the computer. It is possible to have multiple SMART products attached to your computer. If so, you would click on the link for the SMART product you wished to modify tools of.

On the upper right is an Orient button (Orient covered on page 9-10. In the center is a pull down menu, to select a variety of options to control. Here, we will modify the "hard" buttons on the Sympodium interactive monitor. If you have a SMART Board connected, this is where you would modify the colors in the pen tray. For example, you could make the green pen tray become a yellow highlighter of a certain width. Here you can also select the default width of the eraser and the default virtual keyboard you desire.

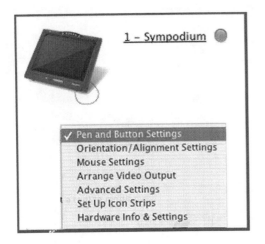

We will cover the important settings options.

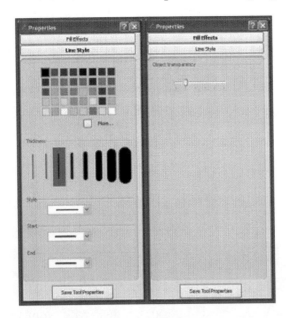

If you wanted to change the green stylus in the pen tray to a yellow highlighter, from the Welcome Center, you would go to the Control Panel, choose your device (SMART Board), click on the Green Pen, and at the Line Style screen (above right), choose a Yellow, and a wider Thickness. You would then touch the Fill Effects tab (above left), move the Object Transparency slider to the right to the fifth notch. Then at the bottom of the screen, click the **Save Tool Settings** button.

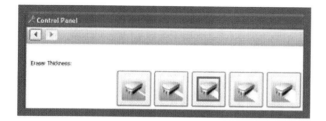

Touch on the Eraser icon to change eraser thickness. At the above screen, touch on the desired thickness, then touch the OK button.

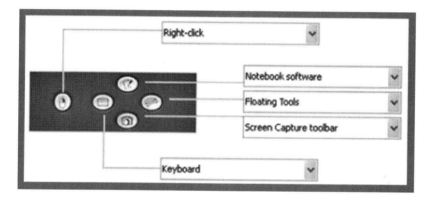

Some SMART products have additional hard buttons. The SMART Sympodium interactive monitor is a 15" or 17" diagonal LCD monitor with SMART Board technology built in. It was originally designed for college lecture halls, because many lecture halls seat 500 or more students. The display size of even the largest SMART Board interactive whiteboard is too small for such a large room, because the students at the back of the room cannot see the image. So, a Sympodium interactive monitor is used at the instructor's podium, where the professor manipulates a computer with a Sympodium interactive monitor and stylus, in the same way we use a SMART Board built into the Sympodium interactive monitor frame.

We use a Symposium interactive monitor as a "personal SMART Board" at our desk for curriculum development. As SMART Boards become more widely used in K-12 schools, we expect to see wider adoption of the AirLiner™ wireless slate and Symposium interactive monitor by district curriculum developers. These "personal interactive whiteboards" are very valuable for e-learning applications.

Select **Orientation/Alignment Settings** from the pull down menu to choose what level of accuracy you desire. If you have used a SMART product for several years, you will remember the 80 point orientation, as an option for graphic artists and computer aided drawing users. Orientation has really improved over the years, but we will show you on page 197, how to add 80 point orientation to this screen. For most of us, even the Quick 4 point orientation works great.

If you change settings on this page, remember to click the Apply button at the bottom right.

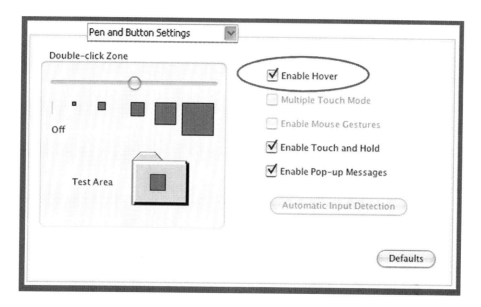

We customize the Mouse Settings by adding **Enable Hover** for the Sympodium interactive monitor or AirLiner wireless slate. As we glide the pen just above the surface, not even touching the glass, the mouse moves with our gesture, giving us better visual feedback of where we are positioned.

This screen also lets you determine how large of an area you want effected with a double click (tapping twice in quick succession in one spot on a SMART product). If you were going to turn a SMART Board into an interactive kiosk, or a language communications board for a special needs student with motor skill challenges, you would select a large double-click sensitivity area.

Some rear-screen SMART products have digital cameras in the corners to sense finger and pen position, and utilize the **Multiple Touch** and **Enable Mouse Gestures** modes. We anticipate seeing this technology built into more SMART products in the future.

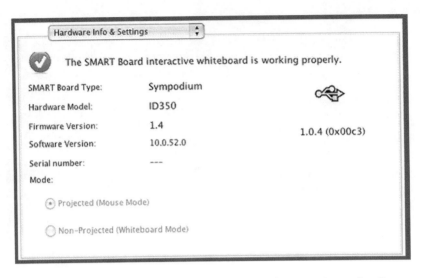

There are several ways to determine what version of software you are using, including this Control Panel Hardware Info area. This is also where you set the SMART Board interactive whiteboard into the Non-Projected mode.

We are often asked if you can write on a SMART Board interactive whiteboard with dry-erase markers. The answer is YES, but clean it right away after use. We found that glass cleaner (like Windex™ from our hometown) works better than anything. We also found that Sanford's Expo Board Doctor™ (UPC code 71641 08504) works great in removing permanent marker (e.g. Sharpie™) applied and cleaned with a paper towel, one square inch at a time, even six months after writing on a SMART Board interactive whiteboard surface.

Once we set up a SMART Board interactive whiteboard in the "non-project mode" for a high school student with macular degeneration (tunnel vision). Even seated at the front of the classroom, she had great difficulty seeing a traditional chalkboard or whiteboard. So, the school's assistive technology specialist prescribed a SMART Board interactive whiteboard, floor stand, and laptop computer. Student volunteers moved this setup from room to room in the high school as she attended different classes. The teachers wrote on the interactive whiteboard with dry-erase markers, and Notebook software recorded the lectures, with the student adding the new Notebook pages just before the teacher erased the interactive whiteboard. This not only aided her considerably in reviewing lecture notes, but enhanced her popularity as students realized that she had electronic lecture notes. You can imagine that she became an expert at "export to PDF."

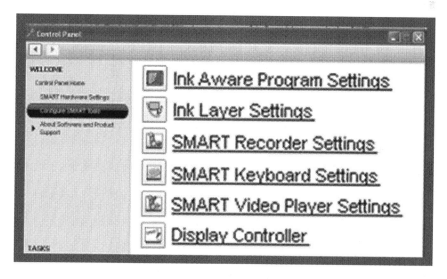

Access this page by touching **Configure SMART Board Software Tools** on the left side of the Control Panel. On the right, click on the tool you wish to configure.

Ink Aware

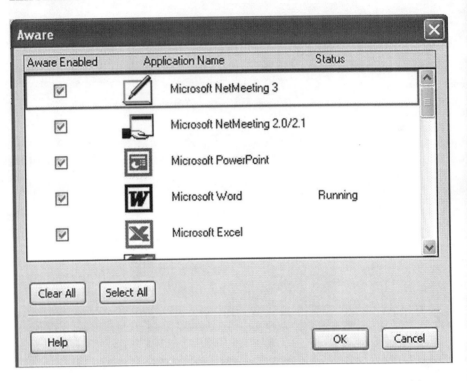

When you click on **Ink Aware Program Settings**, you see this dialog box, which lists all Ink Aware applications, and if it is currently running on your computer in conjunction with SMART Board Tools. You can disable Ink Aware for specific applications by unchecking the Aware Enabled checkboxes.

Current Windows OS Ink Aware applications include: Microsoft Excel, Live Meeting, NetMeeting, Office OneNote, Paint, PowerPoint, Visio, Windows Journal, Word, Corel Draw, Grafigo, Presentations. OpenOffice Calc, Draw, Impress, Writer, Adobe Acrobat Professional, ArcView AutoCAD, AutoView, Volo View, and DWF Composer.

Software developers can purchase SMART's SDK (software developers' toolkit) http://smarttech.com/resourcecenter/sdk/index.asp to add programming code to their applications to create Ink Aware features. Microsoft Word, Excel and PowerPoint are the best known Ink Aware applications.

Crick Software's Clicker Paint is the first educational software that is Ink Aware. Use the pen tray tools to color or erase in this multi-activity coloring book.

Ink Aware applications recognize when you are connected to a SMART Board interactive whiteboard. When you pick up a stylus from the pen tray, the Digital Ink layer does not pop up.

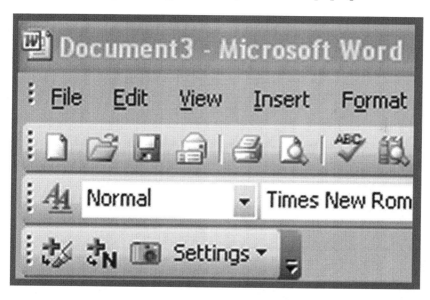

Instead, you see a new **SMART Aware toolbar** in Microsoft Word, with tools for Insert Drawing as Image, Insert Drawing as Text, Capture to Notebook and SMART Aware Settings. Here, you see Microsoft Word 2003. The Ink Aware Toolbar (page 189) is displayed instead in Word 2007.

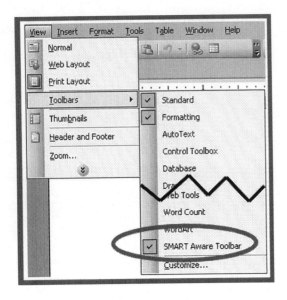

Sometimes those tools are hidden. Your computer must be attached to your SMART Board for the SMART Aware tools to be active. You can then activate them by going to View in Microsoft Word 2003, and pulling down to SMART Aware Toolbar.

In the Ink Aware application, you can also choose View->Customize and click the SMART Aware Toolbar on.

Your students could submit writing to you as Microsoft Word docs. You could then do class analysis on writing assignments. Highlight the text, make the font size large so it is easier to see, and then use the Ink Aware features.

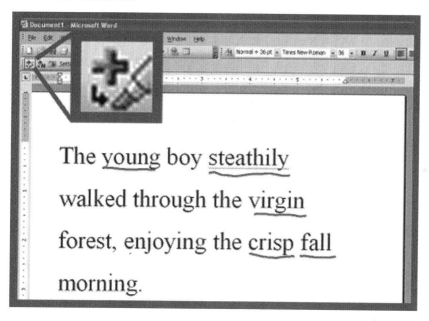

The young boy steathily walked through the virgin forest, enjoying the crisp fall morning.

In this example, underline the adjectives, or better yet, engage the student, by having the author go to the interactive whiteboard and analyze their writing. Once the student has underlined all the adjectives, have her click on the Insert Drawing as Image tool, and the underlining will be imbedded into this Word document.

You can scroll through the Word document and the imbedded annotations will stay with your document vs. using Digital Ink, in which annotations disappear when you touch the SMART Board interactive whiteboard when using your finger as a mouse.

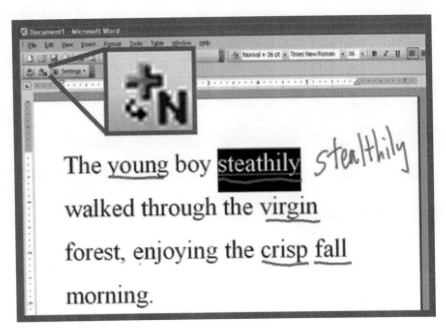

Then have the student correct any spelling mistakes by highlighting each misspelled word and writing it anywhere on the interactive whiteboard. Touch the Insert as Text tool.

The young boy stealthily

walked through the virgin

forest, enjoying the crisp fall

morning.

The handwriting is converted to text, using the stylus color and the font, size and style used in the insert point in the Word document.

Ink Aware lets you enter information directly into Excel spreadsheet cells.

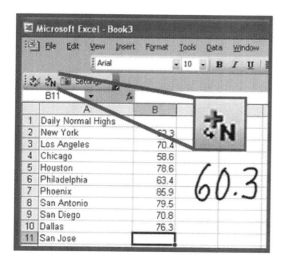

Click on the cell you want to enter information to. Pick up a stylus. Write anywhere on the spreadsheet. Click on the Insert Drawing as Text button. Your handwriting is converted to data.

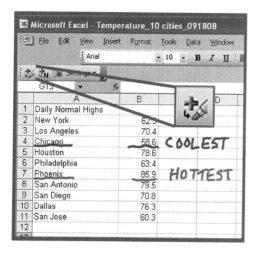

Pick up any stylus. Write over the spreadsheet data. Click on the Insert Drawing as Image button. Your annotation is imbedded in the Excel spreadsheet.

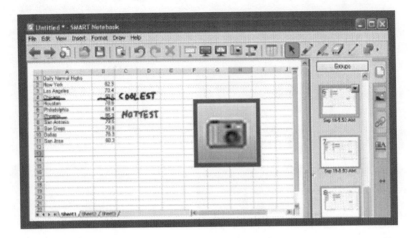

Click on the **Capture to Notebook tool** (Camera) and the exact spreadsheet size you are viewing on your computer is captured to Notebook as a picture.

Clicking on the SMART Aware **Settings** button lets you automatically insert drawing as image.

Ink Aware lets you annotate in the PowerPoint slide show mode and use the Insert as Drawing command to add your handwritten notes to your PowerPoint file.

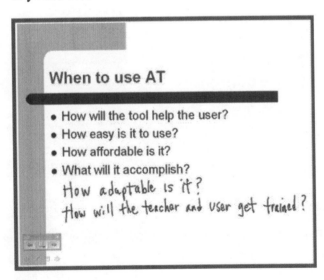

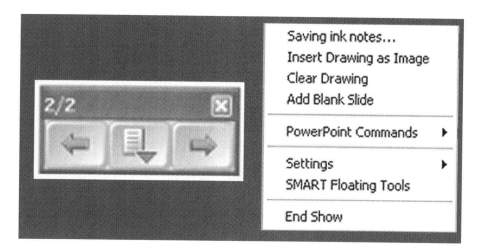

The **SMART Ink Aware Slide Show Toolbar** pops up whenever you are running a PowerPoint Slide Show while your computer is connected to a SMART interactive product (SMART Board interactive whiteboard, Sympodium interactive monitor, AirLiner wireless slate, etc.)

You can navigate to different PowerPoint slides, with the arrow keys or via the Command Menu. If you drag down to **PowerPoint Commands**, you can select **Go to Slide..** and will see all of your PowerPoint slides listed. Simply click on the slide you want to go to.

When you are in the Slide Show mode and you add annotations, you can save just the slides you made annotations to by choosing **Saving Ink Notes**.

Insert Drawing as Image imbeds your annotations into your PowerPoint file.

Restore Drawing / Clear Drawing is an "undo/redo" command to use while you are annotating. You can also use the eraser.

Add Blank Slide does exactly that.

PowerPoint Commands include **Go to Slide** letting you to see a list of slides which you can easily go to, **Black/Unblack Screen** so you can mute the screen, if you want to have the audience focus on something other than the presentation, **Print Slide** and **Show PowerPoint Menu.**

Setup commands are **Double-Press to Advance** (vs. a single press), **Add Drawing at End of Show** (instead of being imbedded in the slide), and **Transparent Toolbar.**

If you turn on **Double-Press to Advance** (the default setting), you can also advance a slide by clicking once on the screen, and again to the right of your first click, and go back a slide by clicking once on the screen, and again to the left of your first click. You want this turned off to make it very easy to advance slides with a single press of the board, for example, for a student with impaired mobility to use.

SMART Floating Tools makes the Floating Toolbar pop up. (We could not get this command to work using Notebook 10 software and PowerPoint 2003.) **End Show** exits you out of the PowerPoint slide show mode.

In PowerPoint, Ink Aware only works in the Slide Show mode, even though a SMART Ink Aware toolbar pops up in the Normal view of PowerPoint.

Ink Layer

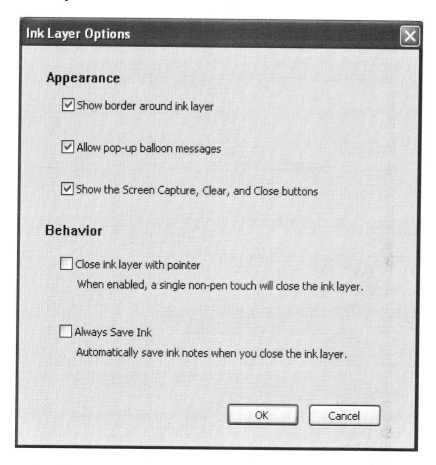

In prior Notebook versions, the **Ink Layer** or the "Digital Ink Layer" was called the "Transparency Mode." When you are using software <u>other</u> than Notebook or Ink Aware applications, and you pick up a stylus from the pen tray, a copy of the screen is captured and layered over your actual display, like a transparency laid on top of your working image. You can then write with electronic ink over this layer, and use Screen Capture to capture images.

Notebook 10 software has some new Ink Layer features. If you want Notebook 10's ink layer to perform the same as Notebook 9's transparency layer, uncheck choice 3 and 5 above. These new features let you more easily capture individual screens and save them into Notebook software, but these features might be confusing to Notebook 9 users.

This screen allows for additional customization. If, for example, you are on the faculty in a teaching hospital, using Notebook software with CT scanning software, and wanted to annotate over brain scan images as seamlessly as possible, you might turn off options 1-3.

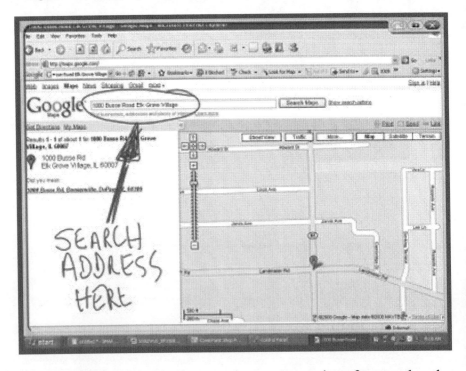

The Digital Ink border lets you know you are in software other than SMART Notebook or Ink Aware software. You can annotate over ANY software, using the SMART Board™ pen tray stylus, or the Floating Tools.

When you have finished writing and use the Select Tool (by putting the stylus in the pen tray and pressing on the interactive whiteboard with your finger, or by getting the Floating Toolbar Select "pointer' tool), you will see a pop-up menu giving you options for saving your annotations.

The upper right corner of the Digital Ink border has three icons: **Clear**, **Screen Capture** and **Close**. As you read on page 191, these buttons can be turned off, if you want a Notebook 9 "Transparency Layer" look.

The middle picture is a close up of the Digital Ink layer pop-up, allowing you to save your annotations into Notebook 10 software. Notebook 10 software will even open up for saving, if needed.

Finally, if you don't save your ink, and bump the board surface, the ink will disappear. However, you will see a **Click here to restore writing** undo button in the lower right corner of your screen, for about three seconds. Touch it and your annotations reappear. If you do not get there in time, click on the Undo icon at the bottom of the Floating Toolbar to retrieve your annotations.

The other SMART Tools will be addressed as follows: SMART
Recorder (page 204-205), SMART Keyboard (page 200-202),
SMART Video Player (page 206-208) and Screen Capture (page 22-
26).

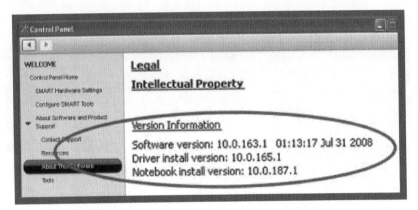

In **About Software and Product Support**, if you click on **About
This Software**, you find the Notebook software version number and
date which SMART Technologies created it. You can also find the
version number if you are running Notebook software on your
Windows computer, under the Help menu, **About Notebook Software**
if you click on the **Technical Support** tab.

You can do some advanced activities in the Tools area. We rarely do these things. **Diagnostics** runs SMART Board Tools which helps highly technical users determine where something might be wrong with their SMART products. You must be connected to the Internet to use the other three options: **Check for Updates** (one of several ways to get updates), **Start Support Session** (allows SMART technical support specialists in Calgary, Canada to do online diagnosis and troubleshooting of your computer/SMART products), and **Register Hardware**, to register your serial numbers online to increase the SMART Board interactive whiteboard warranty from two to five years (other SMART products have different warranty periods).

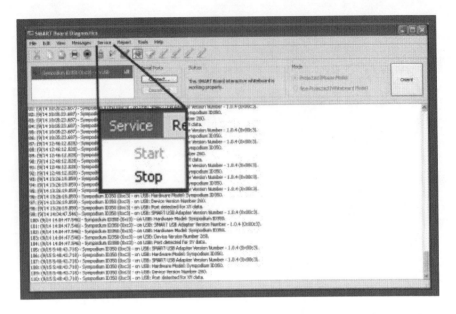

Entering SMART Board diagnostics, you will say "what am I getting into here?" For most people, the best thing to do is go to File and Exit. If you are a district technology specialist or a SMART dealer service representative, you might occasionally venture here, usually while you are on the phone with SMART technical support (1-888-42SMART).

All the displayed text shows each event between your computer and SMART product, including the coordinates which a user touched the board surface.

If, in the rare event that you suspect that an area of a SMART interactive whiteboard is not responding properly, technical support will have you go to this screen and touch on the board. They will ask you to scroll through the displayed menu and give them information on the controller and software being utilized.

We do very strange things with SMART Boards, sometimes interfacing "unsupported" devices together. If we do not get a solid green light on the lower left corner of the SMART Board interactive whiteboard frame, that tells us that the software and hardware are not properly communicating. Sometimes, if we Stop the Service and Restart it, the problem clears up. Again, unless you are a techno-geek, you will probably never do this.

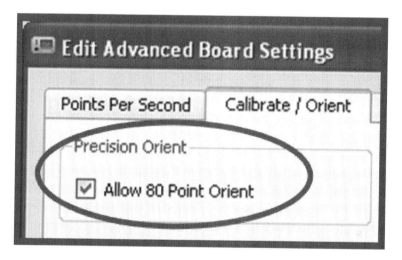

If you want super precision for a CAD application, or some other highly data packed software, you go to the Tools pull down, choose Advanced Board Settings, and click on **Allow 80 Point Precision**. For most users, 9 point orientation is just fine.

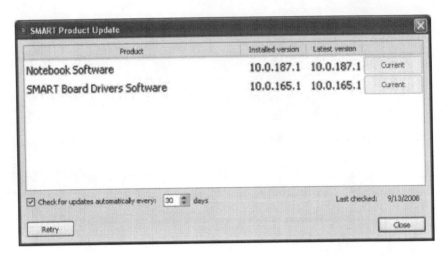

If you **Check for Updates**, you will get this screen. If you are
attached to the Internet, the software goes out to a SMART website,
and lists the Latest version, and you can click to update. If you are a
school IT specialist, you may wish to uncheck the **Check for updates
automatically** checkbox, choosing instead to do manual updates,
using the techniques in the System Administrator Guide. This guide is
available in the Notebook software area of the Support section of
www.smarttech.com/support.

Other SMART Tools

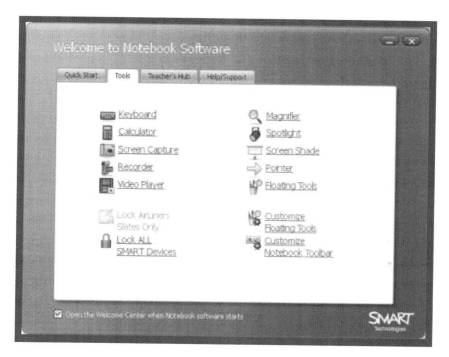

This Welcome Center page shows the **Other SMART Tools**.
These are available from the Open pull down menu in SMART Board
Tools, and most are also accessible via the Floating Toolbar.

SMART Virtual Keyboards

Classic Keyboard

Number Pad Keyboard

Shortcut Keyboard

Simple Keyboard

Simple Caps Keyboard (with Writing line activated)

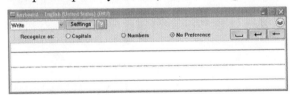

Write Keyboard

You can change the Virtual Keyboard by touching the keyboard pull down menu, and selecting between Classic, Number Pad and Simple. The Simple keyboard can be changed to all capital letters, by touching the shift lock key.

There is also a Write keyboard in the Windows version of SMART Board tools, which allows input via writing on a one line notepad, for handwriting recognition. For example, you could open up a search engine (e.g. Internet Explorer), click on the search box, call up the Virtual Keyboard, and write your search criteria in printed or cursive handwriting. When you stop writing, your handwriting will be converted to text and input into the search box, as if you typed the information in.

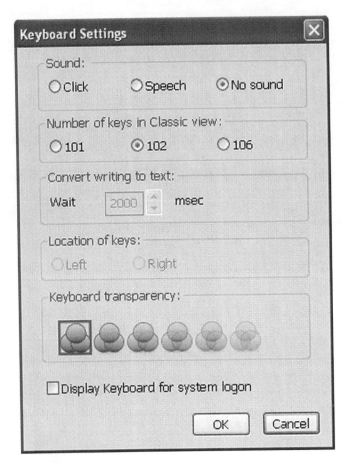

The Virtual Keyboard can be further customized so that it "talks" when you type (Speech) or has a "click" sound, as well as an additional key, or different levels of keyboard transparency so you see your image through the Virtual Keyboard.

You can set the time between when you stop writing on the Write keyboard and when the handwriting is converted to text, in msec (thousands of a second). You can even set up the Virtual Keyboard to be displayed when your system restarts, so you can "type" your user name and password for logon purposes.

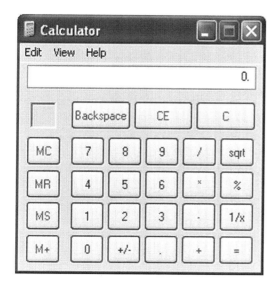

A simple computer **calculator** is also accessible. You can copy and paste from the calculator results window, into Notebook software, by selecting Edit -> Copy, then going into Notebook, selecting the Text tool, and then selecting Edit -> Paste.

The **Screen Capture** tool is extensively discussed on pages 22-26.

SMART Recorder allows you to record any computer images, capture interaction with your SMART product and save this movie. You can even plug a computer microphone into your computer and annotate over the action.

Here we clicked the record button. The recording time and frames per second being recorded is displayed. We can pause (blue pause "equal" sign) or stop (blue square).

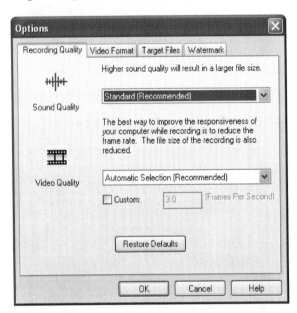

The SMART Recorder's tabs allows you to access **Recording Quality**, **Video Format**, and **Target Files** (tabs at top).

Even though the SMART Recorder on the Windows is saved in the highly compact Windows Media Video (WMV) format, a lesson can consume a large amount of hard drive storage space. You can reduce the file size by changing the Recording Quality, by changing sound and video quality (1 to 5 frames per second) levels. You can even choose Custom and enter up to 10 frames per second.

Another way to reduce file size is to record only an area of your screen. If, for example, you are using Geometer's Sketchpad, and want to record your lecture and interactive calculator, perhaps you just want to select the region around your calculator, not the entire screen, to show formula entry and the shaping of the parabolic curve.

If you want to use record your Notebook software lecture illustrating sentence diagramming, resize the window (grabbing the handle on the lower right corner), plug in your computer microphone, and draw a rectangle around only the active whiteboarding area in Notebook, to keep your file size low. We wouldn't sacrifice audio quality, but might reduce the video frame rate to 1 or 2 frames per second, for that type of lecture.

When finished, you may want to post this lecture to your website or save to a server, for students who need additional repetition.

Video Player

SMART Video Player will play back WMV (Windows Media Video) files. Try these at http://sunearthday.nasa.gov/polarsunrise. Right click on the download.wmv link for "The Aurora" video and save the file to computer storage.

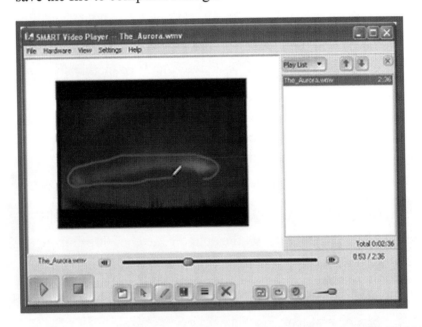

Here you see the Northern Lights highlighted using the SMART Video Player. We used the File command to Open "The Aurora" Windows Media Video file.

SMART Video Player control tools include:

A – Play / Pause ....D – Slider

B – Stop................................E – Next frame

C – Previous frame................F – Volume level

G – Capture to Notebook ....J – Pen color

H – Select pointer..................K – Pen width

I – Pen Tool...........................L – Delete (Restore previous notes)

M – Full Screen toggle...........O – Mute Audio toggle

N – Repeat

We thought it would be interesting to play back a high school football game that was recorded to DVD and use the SMART Video Player to annotate the plays. This is not easy to do. DVD files are recorded as VOB files, and all the VOB files must be put together in order to create a WMV file, which the SMART Video Player reads.

We did this with a Canopus ADVC110 interface box ($279), which converts composite video output from a DVD or VCR player to a Windows Media Player file, and used Windows Movie Maker software to record and edit the football game.

Pinnacle System's Dazzle DVD recorder ($50) is a USB device that can also be used for this purpose.

Using the SMART Video Player would be a great tool for a chemistry teacher. You could record dangerous experiments (mixing potassium and water, working with mercury or hydrochloric acid) and replaying your experiments using the SMART Video Player.

Using the Settings menu, you can even change the playback speed, from very slow (.25x) to very fast (4x).

SMART's Video Player will also play back QuickTime™ movies (MPEG-4).

Hide Floating Tools

Floating Tools is a SMART program which resides on your desktop. Potentially, the Floating Toolbar can have many of the tools discussed in the Tools chapter (pages 11-52). You can move it around by grabbing on the handle, minimize it with the two left triangles, and hide it altogether by going to the SMART Board Tools menu and selecting Hide Floating Tools.

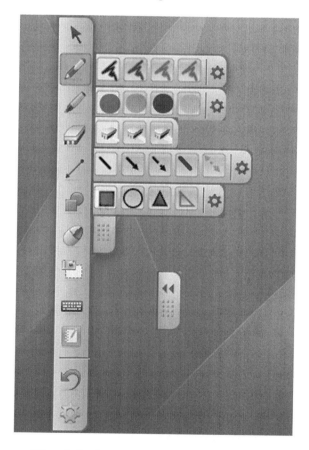

The default Floating Tools can be used to annotate over any software. If you want to change a particular tool (e.g. the rectangle shape, click on the shape, then click on the "gear-widget" icon at the end of the toolbar, to go to Properties.

You can reposition the Floating Toolbar on the screen, by pulling on the dotted area in the pull tab. The two left triangles minimizes the Floating Toolbar, when it is docked at the left or right edge of the screen.

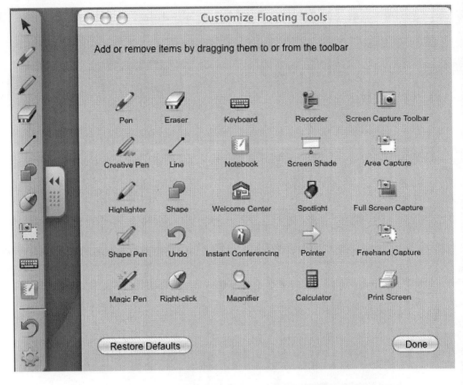

The gear-widget at the bottom of the Floating Toolbar is for Customize Floating Tools. Just drag any tool you desire into or out of the Floating Toolbar, then click the Done button.

Magnifier

There are two areas of the Magnifier; the "lens" window and the "viewing" window. Above is the viewing window. There is a resize handle (three diagonal lines) on the lower right side of the viewing window. There is a gray handle area on top and a control area at the bottom. Point to the top handle area to reposition the Magnify viewing area anywhere on the screen.

The Magnify "viewer" window is at the left, the "lens" frame is at the right, and the resize "cursor" is shown on the lower right corner of the viewer. When you resize the viewer, the lens frame is proportionately resized.

A B C D E F

The Magnify Tools are on the lower left corner of the Viewer:

A – Magnify Using Drag and Drop

B – Magnify Using the Pointer

C – Press Inside Magnifier

D – Show Magnification Lens

E – Spotlight

F – Magnification Level

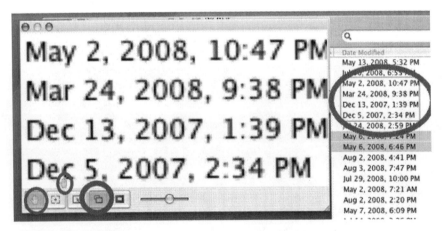

In this example, the red Magnification Frame (D) is shown on the right side, with some file creation dates/times shown in the Viewer window. The Magnify Using Drag and Drop (Hand) is also selected.

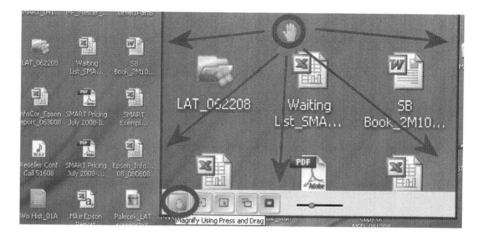

Using the "Magnify Using Drag and Drop" tool, you scroll around the screen, moving the hand around <u>in</u> the viewing window.

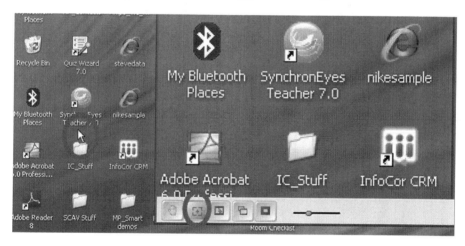

Using the "Magnify Using the Pointer" tool, you scroll <u>outside</u> of the viewing window, pointing to the content you wish to magnify.

Use the "Magnify Using the Spotlight" tool, to turn on the Spotlight, to further highlight the information you are magnifying. Click on the Spotlight icon to turn the Spotlight on or off. You can use the "Magnify Using Drag and Drop" (A), and "Magnify Using the Pointer" (B) in conjunction with both the "Show Magnification Lens" (D) and the "Spotlight" (E) tools.

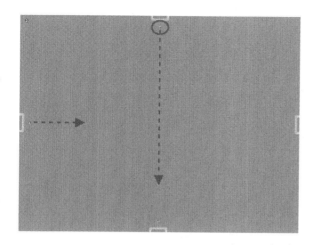

The Screen Shade Tool is like Notebook's Screen Shade tool (page 18), except it works with ANY Windows software program. To reveal content as desired, just pull down on the Screen Shade handles, up OR down and left OR right.

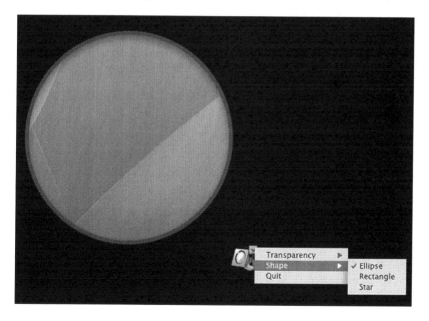

The Spotlight a great way to focus student attention. This is a simple tool to use, with a lot of educational effect, and one of the first you should practice using.

Use the Spotlight with any software. It is more extensive than the Magic Pen spotlight (page 40), because you can pick via the spotlight object menu three different shapes (oval, rectangle, and star) and different transparency levels. Change the spotlight size by touching on the spotlight edge and dragging into or away from the center. Move the spotlight around by touching outside (in the darkened area) and pushing around on the screen.

Trainer Chuck Gevaert uses the rectangular shaped Spotlight with educational websites which have banner "commercials" on them, to block out those distracting banners.

The **Pointer** is not that useful, because it would seem more logical to annotate using a SMART product. For me, the only place it makes sense is in SMART's Bridgit web conferencing software, where there are multiple pointers for each participant to use. If you activate the pointer, right click on it to get rid of it.

Lock All AirLiner Slates Only and Lock All SMART Devices are at the bottom left of the Welcome Center. An AirLiner™ wireless slate is SMART's lowest price "entry level" input device. Manufactured by Wacom for SMART, this is a Bluetooth input pad. You don't need to orient it, and you can have up to seven AirLiners attached to your computer. It can work in conjunction with other SMART products or all by itself.

We use an AirLiner wireless slate, attached to a laptop computer to write curricular content in the living room, at night, while watching television. The laptop screen displays the visual content, while the wireless slate is the input device.

We know teachers who roam their classroom with an AirLiner wireless slate, writing their lecture notes on the wireless slate, displaying the notes on a ceiling mounted projector, saving lecture notes to a learning management system website. AirLiner wireless slates are often used in computer labs, where there are wall-to-wall computers, no room for an interactive whiteboard, and the instructional goal is to use whiteboarding technology to annotate over software for computer application instruction.

An AirLiner wireless slate can be a pass-around tool in the classroom, especially useful for providing technology access to wheelchair bound or otherwise mobility impaired students. If you want to lock the AirLiner out, to prevent a student from writing while someone else is using the interactive whiteboard at the front of the class, just click on **Lock All Airliner Slates Only**.

Occasionally a teacher says "I was using my computer and a student came by, picked up a stylus from the pen tray, and 'scribbled electronic ink' on my grade book." In Notebook 10 software, you can now **Lock Out All SMART Devices** to prevent this. At your computer, use your computer mouse to click on the lock icon to unlock.

Congratulations… by finishing Volume 2, you are now well on your way towards being a SMART Board interactive whiteboard expert. We hope this book provides you the pathway for many highly engaging and interactive experiences in your classroom. Wishing you the best of success!

Index

about SMART Notebook, 120, 194

accents (modern language), 88

add group, 141-142

add page, 11, 15, 20, 81-82

AirLiner™ wireless slate, 178, 217

alignment, 110, 133

allow move, 127

attachments, 15, 76-77, 97, 135, 157-159

Audacity, 100

auto-hide, 14, 79, 80, 122

background, 105, 161, 163

blank page (insert), 89

BMP (Bit Map Picture), 43, 60, 148, 151

bold, 101

Bridgit conferencing software, 216

bring forward, 113

bullets, 46

calculator, 203

capture to Notebook, 183, 188

clear page, 73

Clicker Paint, 183

clock face, 155

clone, 70, 126, 136

close, 193

color, 33, 36-37, 39, 42, 44-45, 49, 90, 105-106, 116, 144, 161, 163, 165-166, 168, 175, 186, 207

communication board, 109

configure SMART Board™ software tools, 13-14

contextual toolbar, 14, 44, 80

control panel, 174-198

copy, 70, 126

creative pen, 12, 20, 34, 114, 161, 170

customize toolbar, 14, 80, 121-122

cut, 70, 126

delete, 12, 16, 32, 70, 126

delete page, 73

diagnostics, 195

digital camera, 179

digital ink, 183, 185, 191-193

document camera, 12, 26-28, 83, 90, 97, 102

draw menu, 111-117

drawing tool, 35-36

dry-erase markers, 180

dual page, 12, 21, 83

DVD, 208

80 point precision, 197

edit groups, 141

edit menu, 69-73

e-learning, 178

eraser, 12, 20, 34-35, 115, 161, 175, 177

Essentials for Educators, 146, 164, 169, 171

exit, 68

export, 57-61

export to PDF, 60-61

extend page, 137

eyedropper, 168

FLV (Flash Video), 95

file menu, 54-68

fill, 13, 20,42, 116, 161

fill effects, 33, 161-168

Flash, 91, 95, 146-148, 153-156

flip, 112, 128

flip a coin, 156

floating tools, 192-193, 209-210

font, 49, 170

foreground color, 37

format menu, 101-110

fraction maker, 48, 155

Froguts, 3

full screen view, 12, 19-20, 80-81

Gallery, 15, 21, 55, 76, 88, 104, 107-109, 133, 135, 146-156, 164, 169, 171

Gallery item file, 55, 96, 148-152

GIF (Compuserve Graphics Interchange), 60

globe, 84

gradient, 38, 105, 165

group, 111, 128, 141-142

handwriting, 87, 124, 201-202

help menu, 118

hide floating tools, 209

HTML, 57-58

hover, 179

image file, 59-60, 62

image fill, 42-43, 105, 167

import, 56-57

infinite clone, 104, 129, 133

Ink Aware, 66, 181-190, 192

ink layer, 181, 191-193

insert blank page, 20

insert drawing as image, 183, 185, 187, 189

insert drawing as text, 183, 186, 187

insert menu, 89-100

insert picture, 90, 161

interactive kiosk, 179

italicize, 44, 101

Jeopardy™, 153

JPG, JPEG, 43, 49, 59, 96, 97, 148, 151, 158

justification, 44

language setup, 85-88

Lesson Activity Toolkit, 127, 134, 156

line, 13, 20, 36, 115, 140, 161

line style, 33, 161, 164-165, 169-170

link, 97-98, 130, 140

lock all Airliner slates only, 217

lock all SMART devices, 217-218

lock in place, 127

locking, 103, 127

magic pen, 13, 20, 40-42, 80-81, 117, 161

magnify, 42, 211-214

magnify glass (Gallery), 149

math symbols, 47-48

Microsoft Excel, 125, 183, 187-188

Microsoft Word, 66, 183-186

more options, 81-82

mouse gestures, 179

MP-10_Simple, 121

MP3, 99-100

multiple touch, 179

My Content folder, 88, 107-108, 144, 146-151

navigation buttons, 156

next page, 11, 15, 78, 81, 84

new, 54

non-project mode, 180

Notebook Tools, 11-51

object animation, 50, 161, 171-172

object menu, 29, 123-134

object transparency, 161, 162

open, 17

open document, 11, 54

order, 113, 129

orient, 9-10, 175, 178

page recording, 51, 161, 173

page setup, 63

page sorter, 15, 75, 135-139

paperclip, 97-98, 157, 158

paste, 12

pattern fill, 37, 105, 166

PDF (portable document file), 60-61, 138, 158

pen, 12, 20, 32-33, 114, 161, 169

pen tray, 10, 175-177

picture file, 89

picture transparency, 102-103, 163

pictures and backgrounds, 146-149

pin page, 14, 21, 83-84

pointer, 216

PowerPoint™, 56-57, 61, 188-190

PNG (Portable Network Graphics), 60

previous page, 11, 15, 78, 81

Promethean Flipchart™, 56-57

print, 62-65

print to Notebook, 65-67

print what, 63

process writing, 137-139

properties, 13, 15, 32-33, 39, 42, 49-50, 77, 101, 131, 135, 151-152, 160-173

Public.Resource.org, 96

QuickTime™, 208

question and answer, 153

recognize handwriting, 124

recognize shapes, 125

recognize table, 125

redo, 12, 16, 70

register hardware, 195

resize, 31, 43, 45, 60, 133, 137, 147, 154, 164, 205, 211

resize handle, 29-30

rolling dice, 153

Sanford Expo Board Doctor™, 180

save, 17, 55

save document, 11, 55

save page as Gallery item, 55

save tool, 33, 167, 177

SCORM, 55

screen capture, 12, 22-26, 78, 111, 192-193

screen shade, 12, 18, 20, 79, 142, 215

search Gallery, 147-149

search results, 147, 149

select, 12, 20, 32, 36, 80-81, 113, 193

select all, 72

select all locked notes, 72

send back, 114

send to, 68

Senteo™ response system, 63, 92-94

shapes, 13, 20, 37-38, 42, 116

shape recognition, 13, 39, 42

show all links, 84-84

size, 44, 170

slide sorter view, 59-60

SMART Aware Settings, 183-184

SMART Keyboard, 45, 181

SMART Recorder, 14, 181, 204-205

SMART Tools, 195-198

SMART Video Player, 14, 181, 206-208

sound, 99-100, 130

spelling, 48, 71

special needs student, 101, 109, 179, 190

split cells, 131-132

spotlight, 40, 215

start / end, 161

style, 44, 161, 170

stylus, 4, 7, 10, 16, 32-33, 113, 123, 176-177, 183, 186-187, 191-193, 218

subscript, 47

superscript, 47

support session, 195

SVG (scalable vector graphics), 58-59

SWF (Shockwave Flash), 91, 95

Sympodium™, 175-180

System Administrators' Guide, 198

table, 12, 18, 29-31, 45, 100, 131-134

technical support (SMART), 120, 196

technical support (tab), 120

text, 20, 44-48, 70, 117, 161, 170

themes, 106-109, 143-145

thickness, 161

thumbnails, page sorter, 136-139

TIF, TIFF, 43

timed saves, 62

timer, 154

title pages, 136, 140

toggle dual screen, 12

toggle toolbar, 13, 52

tool menu, 199

tools (advanced), 199

transparency, 36-37, 42, 77, 79, 93, 161-163, 176, 191-193, 202, 216

underline, 101

undo, 12, 16, 20, 69, 80-81, 193

unfilled shape, 38

ungroup, 111

updates, 119, 195, 198

URL (universal resource locator), 25, 77, 98, 158-159

use small size, 122

vector, 35-36, 39

version, 120, 194

vertical text tool, 45

view menu, 74-88

virtual keyboard, 10, 17, 45, 175, 200-202

virtual control (right mouse) click, 10

VOB file, 208

web browser, 159

web page, 57-59

Welcome Center, 8-10, 174

Windex™, 180

WMV (Windows Media Video), 158, 206

zoom, 14

Simple SMART™ Skills

http://smarttech.com/trainingcenter/windows/trainingmaterials.asp, 15

www.tlfe.org.uk/promethean/flipcharts, 56

www.adobe.com/svg/viewer/install, 58

http://www.starr.net/is/type/kbh.html, 88

www.leconcombre.com/board/dl/us/Calmbay1us.html, 91

http://edtechninja.com/smartboard/ask-the-tech-ninja-1-flash-video#comment-42, 95

http://bulk.resource.org/si.edu, 96

http://www.flickr.com/photos/publicresourceorg/collections/72157600
214199993, 96

http://stores.lulu.com/publicresource, 96

www.a1freesoundeffects.com, 99

www.audacity.sourceforge.net, 100

http://www.wpclipart.com, 151

http://smarttech.com/resourcecenter/sdk/index.asp, 183

http://www.smarttech.com/support, 198

http://sunearthday.nasa.gov/polarsunrise, 206

4441980

Made in the USA
Lexington, KY
26 January 2010